The CANNY COOK

PHIL VICKERY

The CANNY COOK

FREEZER + STORECUPBOARD
meals on a budget

KYLE BOOKS

An Hachette UK Company
www.hachette.co.uk

First published in Great Britain in 2022
by Kyle Books, an imprint of
Octopus Publishing Group Limited
Carmelite House
50 Victoria Embankment
London EC4Y 0DZ

ISBN: 978 1 91423 911 3

Publishing Director: **Judith Hannam**
Publisher: **Joanna Copestick**
Editor: **Claire Rogers**
Editorial Assistant: **Zakk Raja**
Design: **Helen Bratby**
Photography and props styling: **Kate Whitaker**
Food styling: **Jules Mercer**
Production: **Katherine Hockley**

A Cataloguing in Publication record for this
title is available from the British Library.

Printed and bound in Italy

10 9 8 7 6 5 4 3 2 1

FSC MIX
Paper from
responsible sources
FSC® C015829
www.fsc.org

CONTENTS

INTRODUCTION

The idea for this book first occurred to me more than thirty years ago. I had taken a job as a head chef running a very busy hotel/restaurant/brasserie just as the country was hit by a deep recession. I had grown used to the excesses of the 1980s, and in the restaurants where I had worked previously, money had never seemed to be a problem. Overseas visitors, especially from the US, spent lavishly – Champagne, caviar and lobster were the norm – but that was all about to change.

On the day I walked into the job, the accountant told me that the hotel was in deep financial trouble and that we had six months to turn things around or they would have to shut the doors. I lost many of the kitchen staff; the expensive ingredients I had become accustomed to went out the window; and menus were scaled right back to the bare minimum. It was a huge shock.

I had to completely rethink my approach to everything, and tailor the dishes to the ingredients I could afford, not what I necessarily wanted to cook. I started to look at canned and frozen foods such as pulses, beans and tomatoes purely as a way to avoid wastage and even (I'm not ashamed to admit) used Maggi stock powders to avoid a hefty gas bill for twelve hours of simmering bones.

Not long after I'd been there, a well-known food critic, accompanied by an equally well-known chef, came to the restaurant and had a three-course lunch. The starter was butterbean and thyme soup – made using just onions, canned butterbeans, dried thyme, water and olive oil. As soon as they'd finished it, the head waiter came rushing into the kitchen to say that they had enjoyed it so much they'd like another bowl! The following week, the critic's review appeared in a national newspaper. In it, he praised the soup, saying what a lovely depth of flavour it had. It made me realise that if a serious foodie was happy with canned produce, we could just carry on. On another occasion, a head inspector from a world-renowned food guide came for dinner. I can't remember his starter, but his main course was a frozen (by me) chicken, with braised (canned) chickpeas and dessert was a steamed sponge pudding with syrup, custard and clotted cream. I made the custard from good old Bird's powder and finished it with Lyle's Golden Syrup. Lo and behold, the next year I was awarded a Michelin star. And I wasn't alone. A three-star Michelin chef of the time used canned peaches (which I adore) in a warm soufflé and charged £16 for it – a lot of money back in the early nineties!

The reason I tell you all of this is that for many years now I have been happy to use frozen and canned products, as the quality is hard to beat. I have been criticised by fellow chefs for 'deskilling' the industry, but my view is quite simple: if the flavour and texture is just as good – and it's cheaper – why wouldn't you use canned or frozen? I use the example of the humble frozen pea. That pea is harvested, cooked and frozen within two hours of being picked, locking in all its vitamins and nutrients. The freezing process still allows enzymes to slowly turn starch into sugar, which is why frozen peas are always sweet. I don't know one chef who doesn't use them.

In France, a place with a rich culinary history, there is no such snobbery about preserved food. Canned confit duck, foie gras, vegetables, fruit, bouillabaisse, etc. are all seen as high quality and are revered. Many top French chefs over the years have developed high-quality frozen food lines in all the major supermarkets and have been very successful.

Italy is the same. I've spent a good few years visiting a huge factory there that makes Italian sauces for the UK market and have never seen a fresh tomato being used. One day I asked the head development chef why they didn't use fresh tomatoes. He looked at me in disbelief, shrugged his shoulders and said, 'They don't

have a deep enough flavour.' They also used triple concentrate tomato purée, which is almost purple in colour.

As soon as lockdown occurred, people started to panic buy as if we were about to undergo a nuclear attack. Supermarkets were cleared out of fresh produce with quite astonishing speed. I would wander in to get my weekly shop and look at what was left: usually things such as canned potatoes, canned tuna, mackerel and pilchards, and canned peaches, pears and pineapple. But then they all started to go, too, largely, I think, because there was nothing else to buy. People often wrongly assume that frozen and canned foods are not as nutritious as fresh produce, not realising that using them often cuts down, or eliminates entirely, the preservatives that are added to many so-called 'fresh' products to give them extra 'shelf life'. Using canned and frozen food – which, after all, is so convenient – can make achieving your five-a-day a doddle and can also, as I show in these pages, form the basis of some surprisingly tasty, easy dishes.

Canning and freezing processes have come a long way since Nicolas Appert, a French chemist and chef, began looking at bottling and canning foods in the mid-1700s and since the now-famous Mr Birdseye pioneered frozen foods in the early 1900s. (If you want to know more, read Sue Shephard's brilliant book, *Pickled, Potted & Canned*.) Now there are sophisticated industries that produce nutritious food that is both easy to use and store, and extremely good value for money. The number of renowned chefs working with canned and frozen food manufacturers is testament to their high quality.

Frozen and canned fish have come on in leaps and bounds. Frozen tuna, salmon and bass are amazing quality. Canned crab, squid in black sauce and smoked oysters make a nice change to the daily foods on offer. I love frozen fruit such as raspberries, pineapple, blackcurrants and mango. Likewise canned peaches are superb, as are canned pears, lychees and even strawberries. Pulses, beans and vegetables all freeze really well – I adore frozen baby broad beans, peas, mixed vegetables and thrice-cooked frozen chips! Frozen rice sachets are great as are frozen mashed potatoes, hash browns, waffles and even giant Yorkshire puds. Huge butterbeans canned in tomato sauce are a favourite of mine from years of going to Greece, and so are canned stuffed vine leaves. Baked beans are, of course, a staple, but even I draw the line at an all-day breakfast in a can.

SO, ALL IN ALL, USING CANNED & FROZEN FOOD IS A NO-BRAINER AS FAR AS I'M CONCERNED, AS IT:

Doesn't mean compromising on flavour.

Can contribute to your five-a-day.

Is an easy way to increase your fish intake.

Allows you to get more for your money.

Means you always have something to hand with which to make a quick and easy meal.

STORECUPBOARD ESSENTIALS

What follows is a list of the items that I have pretty much all the time at home in either the cupboard or the freezer. It's only a guide, but next time you're out and about, have a quick look; I think you'll be surprised at the variety available, plus you'll save a few quid – I certainly did when I decided to write this book!

- Canned lentils and peas: green lentils, chickpeas, black-eyed peas.
- Canned beans: butterbeans, borlotti, kidney and cannellini beans, and good old baked beans.
- Tomatoes: canned whole or chopped tomatoes in juice, sometimes with herbs; sun-dried or sun-blush tomatoes; passata; and tomato purée.
- Other canned and jarred vegetables: asparagus, olives, peppers, potatoes, pumpkin and sweetcorn.
- Meat: canned or vacuum-packed hot dogs; Spam; canned corned beef.
- Canned fish: anchovies, crab, mackerel, salmon and tuna.
- Fruit: canned fruit such as cherries, peaches, pears, pineapple and prunes; dried fruit and nuts such as apricots, chopped roasted hazelnuts and roasted peanuts.
- Tomato soup: a good snack, but also a good base for a stew, stir-fry or braise.

- Rice and pasta: dried macaroni and fusilli; instant rice noodles. Plus microwaveable rice and pulses are great value and super convenient.
- Oils: olive, sesame, sunflower, vegetable. Low-flavour oils such as sunflower, rapeseed and vegetable oil are really good for a neutral flavour. I tend to use perfumed oils such as extra virgin olive oil only for finishing dishes or salads when little or no cooking is needed.
- Sauces: soy, fish and Worcestershire sauces; vinegar; mayo and salad cream; mustard; tomato and brown sauces; Sriracha.
- Flavourings and seasonings: salt and pepper, of course; crumbly stock cubes; dried garlic granules, onion powder and celery salt; pastes such as miso, harissa and pesto.
- Dried herbs and spices: oregano, chilli flakes, ground cinnamon, ground cloves, ground cumin, ground nutmeg, paprika and smoked paprika. Also dried panko breadcrumbs are handy.
- Baking: baking powder and bicarb; cornflour; plain and self-raising flour; yeast.
- Spreads and sweet things: chocolate; custard powder; condensed and evaporated milks; golden syrup and runny honey; jam, marmite and peanut butter; sugar.

And FREEZER ESSENTIALS

- Potatoes: hash browns, waffles, mashed potato, roast potatoes and sweet potato.
- Veg: broad beans, green beans, Brussels sprouts, cauliflower florets, chopped onions, peas, sliced peppers, spinach and sweetcorn.
- Meat: chicken pieces; cooked duck legs; mince and burgers (some even made from venison, wagyu and rose veal!); pork ribs. Even frozen Peking duck with sauce and pancakes can be really good quality.
- Fish: crab, tuna, salmon, raw and cooked prawns, mixed seafood and good old fish fingers.
- Frozen fruit: blackcurrants, blueberries, mango and raspberries.
- Herbs and spices: chilli, coriander, basil, parsley and ginger are superb.
- Pastry: ready-rolled puff, shortcrust and filo are handy.

QUICK FIXES

OVERNIGHT OATS 3 WAYS

BASIC OVERNIGHT OATS

SERVES
2

PREP *5 minutes*
CHILLING *overnight*

These overnight oats are so versatile; you can choose almost any topping you like. These other ideas all work really well:

▶ Frozen fruits of the forest
▶ Frozen mango chunks
▶ Canned strawberries
▶ Canned prunes

50g rolled oats
150ml any milk
3–4 tablespoons water
1 tablespoon runny honey

1. In a bowl, mix all the ingredients together really well.

2. Cover and pop in the fridge overnight. Stir occasionally.

CARROT CAKE OATS

SERVES
2

PREP **15** *minutes*
CHILLING *overnight*

50g rolled oats
150ml any milk
3–4 tablespoons water
1 tablespoon runny honey
1 small carrot, finely grated, plus extra to serve
½ teaspoon ground cinnamon
finely grated zest of 1 small lemon
2–3 tablespoons chopped roasted skinned
    hazelnuts, plus extra to serve

1. In a bowl, mix the oats, milk, water and honey really well.

2. Stir in the carrot, cinnamon and lemon zest and mix well.

3. Chill in the fridge overnight.

4. Just before serving, stir through the hazelnuts and top with a few more, plus a little grated carrot.

RASPBERRY, APPLE & BLUEBERRY OATS

SERVES
2

PREP **15** *minutes*
CHILLING *overnight*

50g rolled oats
150ml any milk
3–4 tablespoons water
1 tablespoon runny honey
100g frozen raspberries
1 small apple, grated
100g fresh or frozen blueberries

1. In a bowl, mix the oats, milk, water and honey really well.

2. Spoon one third of the mix into a bowl, then add the raspberries.

3. Top with another third of the oats, then add the grated apple.

4. Finally add the remaining oats and chill in the fridge overnight.

5. Just before serving, top with the blueberries.

Basic overnight oats PAGE 16

Carrot cake oats PAGE 17   *Raspberry, apple & blueberry oats* PAGE 17

SWEETCORN SALAD

SERVES
2

PREP **5 minutes**
COOKING **none**

make ahead

vegetarian

340g can good-quality sweetcorn, well drained
  (285g drained weight)
4 tablespoons salad cream
2 tablespoons mayonnaise
salt and freshly ground black pepper

When I was a young lad in the early seventies, KFC opened a shop in my home town. It was all a bit new for us, so my dad would take us there for a birthday treat. Yep. Once a year. I distinctly remember not only the fried chicken but also the barbecue spare ribs they used to sell, which were absolutely delicious. We always got a sweetcorn salad with the meal, and I've always liked it. So here is my version, and it's pretty close to the one I ate some fifty years ago.

1. Mix all the ingredients together well in a bowl and then serve.

SIMPLE TOMATO SALSA

SERVES
4

PREP **10** *minutes*
COOKING *none*

make ahead

vegan

400g can chopped tomatoes with
   herbs in juice
1 small red onion, very finely chopped
4 tablespoons extra virgin olive oil
2 tablespoons vinegar, or more to taste
2 tablespoons sugar, or more to taste
salt and freshly ground black pepper

A very easy tomato salsa, the only real secret
is adding vinegar and sugar to balance
the acidity. I sometimes add fresh basil for
another flavour profile. It can be served hot
or cold.

1. Drain the tomatoes well, reserving their juice.

2. Place all the other ingredients into a bowl
and mix well.

3. Add just enough juice to make a thick relish.
Check the seasoning and adjust if needed with
more salt, ground pepper, sugar and/or vinegar.

CHEESE, SPINACH & EGG TOASTIE

SERVES
2

PREP **5 minutes**
COOKING **5–6 minutes**

A few years ago toasties were all the rage, and I have always liked them as a quick fix. Here are a few examples of how they have changed over the years from the bog-standard cheese and tomato. I use a toastie machine, but if you don't have one, you can use a non-stick frying pan lined with greaseproof paper over a medium heat: place the sandwich in the lined pan, then place another piece of greaseproof paper on top and lightly press down using another pan as a weight. Once the bottom is cooked, remove the top pan, flip over the toastie and cook on the other side.

4 slices of bread
1 tablespoon softened butter
4 slices any cheese
2 eggs
handful of baby spinach leaves
dash of Worcestershire sauce

1. Butter the bread and then place two slices butter-side down in a toastie maker.

2. Lay a slice of cheese on each slice of bread, then crack the eggs on top.

3. Add a few spinach leaves and a dash of Worcestershire sauce, then place the remaining slices of cheese on top.

4. Top with the remaining two slices of bread, butter-side up.

5. Press and cook for 5–6 minutes.

LOBSTER & MACARONI CHEESE TOASTIE

SERVES
2

PREP **5** *minutes*
COOKING **5–6** *minutes*

4 slices of bread
1 tablespoon softened butter
4 thin slices macaroni cheese (see page 58)
150g canned lobster or crab

1. Butter the bread and then place two slices butter-side down in a toastie maker.

2. Lay one thin slice of macaroni cheese on each slice of bread. Add the lobster or crab, then top with a further slice of macaroni cheese.

3. Top with the remaining two slices of bread, butter-side up.

4. Press and cook for 5–6 minutes.

BANOFFEE TOASTIE

SERVES
2

PREP **5** *minutes*
COOKING **5–6** *minutes*

vegetarian

4 slices of bread
1 tablespoon softened butter
2 small or 1 large banana(s), peeled, then roughly chopped
2–3 tablespoons toffee sauce
salt and freshly ground black pepper

1. Butter the bread and then place two slices butter-side down in a toastie maker.

2. Spoon on the chopped banana and then drizzle over the toffee sauce. Sprinkle with a little salt and pepper.

3. Top with the remaining two slices of bread, butter-side up.

4. Press and cook for 5–6 minutes.

MORE TOASTIE RECIPES →

5 WAYS WITH TOASTIES

HAM & CHEESE TOASTIE

SERVES
2

PREP **5** *minutes*
COOKING **5-6** *minutes*

4 slices of bread
1 tablespoon softened butter
2 thick slices of Cheddar
2 thick slices of cooked ham
English mustard
freshly ground black pepper

1. Butter the bread and then place two slices butter-side down in a toastie maker.

2. Lay a slice of cheese on each slice of bread. Add the ham, then a dash of mustard and a little pepper.

3. Top with the remaining two slices of bread, butter-side up.

4. Press and cook for 5–6 minutes.

CHICKEN TIKKA, MINT & RED ONION TOASTIE

SERVES
2

PREP **5** *minutes*
COOKING **5-6** *minutes*

4 slices of bread
1 tablespoon softened butter
150g cooked chicken tikka
4 tablespoons mayonnaise
2 tablespoons freshly chopped mint
¼ red onion, thinly sliced
2 teaspoons mango chutney
2 tablespoons freshly chopped coriander

1. Butter the bread and then place two slices butter-side down in a toastie maker.

2. In a bowl, mix the rest of the ingredients except the coriander together well and then spread onto the two slices of bread. Add the coriander on top.

3. Top with the remaining two slices of bread, butter-side up.

4. Press and cook for 5–6 minutes.

SAUSAGE ROLL

MAKES
24

PREP **20** *minutes plus chilling*
COOKING **20–25** *minutes*

make ahead

FOR THE FILLING

500g good-quality (15–20% fat) sausage meat

150g dried apricots, finely chopped

100g vacuum-packed or canned chestnuts,
    finely chopped

2 tablespoons freshly chopped sage

FOR THE PASTRY

500g frozen ready-rolled puff pastry, defrosted

1 egg, beaten

I like sausage rolls, when they are not soggy, fatty or undercooked. Here is a nice recipe that I sometimes cook at Christmas, but they are really good all year around. The sweetness of the dried fruits and the texture of the chestnuts are a real nice part of these beauties. If you have any pastry left over, just refreeze to use another day.

1. Preheat the oven to 200°C/gas mark 6.

2. In a bowl, mix all the ingredients for the filling together well.

3. Unroll the defrosted pastry on a board and cut into 10cm-wide strips. Brush well with some of the beaten egg.

4. Using a piping bag, pipe the sausage meat, slightly to one side, along the strips. Fold over and seal the edges well with your fingers.

5. Brush again with beaten egg, then chill in the fridge for at least 15 minutes.

6. Cut into small rolls, then place on a baking tray. Bake in the oven for 20–25 minutes until browned, crisp and cooked through.

BASIC HOT DOG

SERVES
2

PREP **5 minutes**
COOKING **5-10 minutes**

I'm a real lover of canned or vacuum-packed hot dog sausages. I think they must be a throwback to my younger days when Mum would cook with canned foods like Spam and corned beef. When I was growing up, they were seen as a staple part of the diet. Yes, you could argue that they are not particularly good for you, and they shouldn't be eaten every day, but as an occasional treat, they can form part of a balanced diet.

GENERAL TIPS

▶ Always cook sausages slowly; this ensures they do not split or explode.
▶ Add a little oil to stop them scorching.
▶ Do not overcook or the texture will be dry and rough.
▶ Try slowly pan-frying them, then finishing under a grill or in a moderate oven.
▶ You can cook them the day before, leave to cool, chill in the fridge and then reheat when they are needed.

4 hot dogs
4 hot dog rolls
tomato ketchup, to taste
yellow mustard, to taste
pickled jalapeños, to taste

I. Simply warm the hot dogs according to the packet instructions, then place each into a hot dog roll.

2. Top with ketchup, yellow mustard and/or pickled jalapenos as you like!

BRITISH HOT DOG

SERVES
2

PREP **5** *minutes*
COOKING **10-15** *minutes*

4 Cumberland sausage rings
4 bread rolls (bap/barn or huffkin)
1 quantity Apple Juice Onions (see right)
English mustard, to taste

I. Cook the Cumberland rings according to the packet instructions, then place each into a roll.

2. Top with the onions and English mustard.

APPLE JUICE ONIONS

SERVES
4

PREP **10** *minutes*
COOKING **30** *minutes*

4 tablespoons any oil
4 onions, sliced
1 tablespoon finely chopped fresh or dried sage
350ml apple juice
salt and freshly ground black pepper

I. Heat the oil in a pan over a high heat and add the onions. Fry for 2–3 minutes to get some colour on them.

2. Turn down the heat and then add the sage and juice. Cook down for 10 minutes until you have a thick stew.

3. Season well with salt and pepper.

MORE HOT DOG RECIPES →

MERGUEZ HOT DOG

SERVES
4

PREP **10 *minutes***
COOKING **10-15 *minutes***

4 merguez sausages
4 pittas
1 quantity Cabbage & Mint Salad (see right)
4 heaped tablespoons mayo
1 tablespoon harissa paste

I. Cook the sausages according to the packet instructions.

2. Meanwhile, in a bowl mix together the mayo and harissa paste well.

3. Fill a pitta with the cabbage salad, then add the sausage and top with the mayo.

CABBAGE & MINT SALAD

SERVES
2

PREP **1 *hour***
COOKING ***none***

250g red or white cabbage, very finely sliced
    (ideally using a Japanese mandolin)
1 garlic clove, finely chopped
3 tablespoons extra virgin olive oil
2 tablespoons any vinegar
2 good pinches of caster sugar
4 tablespoons freshly chopped mint
salt and freshly ground black pepper

I. In a bowl, mix all the ingredients together really well, then set aside, ideally for 1 hour if you can.

SPAM FRITTERS
WITH SPRING ONION MASH

SERVES
4

PREP **10** *minutes*
COOKING **15** *minutes*

500g frozen mashed potatoes
200ml milk
50g salted butter
4 spring onions, finely chopped
vegetable oil, for deep-frying
340g can Spam, chilled
300ml sparkling water
200g self-raising flour
2–3 tablespoons cornflour

I had to include my version of this iconic school food staple. I vividly remember seeing the large aluminium trays stacked full of Spam fritters in the canteen. Every shop in my town served them in some way, shape or form. They're real marmite things: you either love them or hate them. I hope this recipe brings back a few memories.

1. Reheat the mash in a microwave-safe bowl according to the packet instructions and mix well.

2. Add the milk and butter, and then microwave for a few seconds to melt the butter. Mix well and taste for seasoning. Stir in the spring onions and set aside.

3. Heat the vegetable oil in a deep pan or wok to 180°C. Cut the Spam into four equal slices.

4. Place the flour in a bowl, add the sparkling water to the flour and then mix into a soft batter. Dust each slice of Spam with a little cornflour, then dip into the batter.

5. Carefully slide into the hot oil and cook for 4–5 minutes until browned and crispy.

6. Drain well on kitchen paper. Serve with the spring onion mash.

SPAM & PEA RICE

SERVES
4

PREP **10** *minutes*
COOKING **25** *minutes*

3 tablespoons olive oil
1 small onion, very finely chopped
200g long-grain rice
200g can Spam, finely chopped
200g frozen peas
400ml boiling water
2 × 10g chicken stock cubes, crumbled
1 tablespoon cold salted butter, cubed
salt and freshly ground black pepper

I make no apology whatsoever for occasionally using a can of Spam – or corned beef for that matter. I was brought up on the stuff and I remember the texture and flavour as if it was yesterday. In this dish it imparts a really nice flavour in the rice. Oh, and by the way, Spam is used in Hawaii's national dish.

1. Preheat the oven to 200°C/gas mark 6.

2. Heat the oil in an ovenproof, non-stick frying pan over a medium heat. Add the onion and fry for 2 minutes.

3. Add the rice and coat well with the oil and onions, then add the Spam and peas. Add enough of the boiling water to just cover the meat, veg and rice.

4. Sprinkle in the stock cubes, stir and then bring back to the boil.

5. Cover the frying pan and place in the oven. Cook for 14 minutes.

6. Once cooked, stir well and then add the butter and season. Leave to stand, covered, for 5 minutes before serving.

BAKED SWEET POTATO, BACON & HONEY OATS

SERVES
4

PREP **10 minutes**
COOKING **25 minutes**

MAKE AHEAD
freezable

MAKE VEGETARIAN
by swapping bacon for nuts

An unusual breakfast offering that can be made well in advance and can be either chilled or frozen. You can omit the bacon if you wish; add pecans or hazelnuts instead.

8 rashers streaky bacon, cut into
    small pieces
1 tablespoon any oil
250g frozen sweet potato cubes
150g rolled oats
½ teaspoon baking powder
200ml any milk
2 tablespoons runny honey

1. Preheat the oven to 180°C/gas mark 4. Line a deep 20cm baking tray with greaseproof paper.

2. Place the bacon and oil into a frying pan over a medium heat and cook for 2–3 minutes until crispy. Remove the bacon with a slotted spoon and set aside. Add the sweet potato, then reduce the heat to low. Cover with a piece of foil and cook for 10 minutes until soft.

3. Place the oats in a bowl, add the baking powder and mix well.

4. Once the sweet potato is cooked, spoon onto a plate, then gently mash with a fork. Mix the sweet potato, milk and honey together really well. Stir into the oats and mix really well.

5. Spoon into the lined baking tray. Spoon over the bacon pieces and gently press in.

6. Bake in the oven for 20 minutes or until nicely browned and slightly puffed.

7. Remove from the oven, carefully lift out of the pan with the greaseproof paper and leave to cool a little. Cut and eat.

SMOKED CHICKEN, TOMATO & PEA PAN PIE

SERVES
4

PREP **15** *minutes*
COOKING **40-45** *minutes*

No faffing about: just line an ovenproof frying pan with filo, bake, fill, top and bake again. The base is nice and crisp, and the filling is hearty and tasty. Pretty much any filling can be used, but the drier the fillings, the better the pie.

10 sheets frozen filo pastry, roughly defrosted
1 egg, beaten
25–30g butter, melted
4 tablespoons olive oil, plus extra for drizzling
1 onion, finely chopped
1 courgette, finely chopped
1 garlic clove, crushed
400g can chopped tomatoes in juice
200g frozen peas
10g beef stock cube, crumbled
400g smoked chicken breast, roughly chopped
1 teaspoon smoked paprika
4 tablespoons chopped fresh parsley (about a small bunch)
salt and freshly ground black pepper
green salad, to serve (optional)

1. Preheat the oven to 200°C/gas mark 6.

2. Place a few sheets of filo pastry in a 20cm × 3cm-deep, ovenproof, non-stick frying pan, brushing each layer with a little beaten egg and then melted butter. Keep any trimmings for the top later.

3. Bake in the oven for 10 minutes to set the egg and pastry, then remove.

4. Meanwhile, heat the oil in a saucepan over a high heat. Add the onion, courgette and garlic and cook for 10 minutes to soften.

5. Add the tomatoes, peas and stock cube and simmer for 12–15 minutes until nice and thick.

6. Stir in the chicken and season well with salt and pepper. Spoon into the cooked filo.

7. Very finely slice the rest of the filo pastry and place into a bowl. Drizzle with olive oil, sprinkle over the smoked paprika and chopped parsley, then season well.

8. Arrange the filo on top of the filled pie. Pop into the oven and bake for a further 15 minutes until nicely browned. Serve with green salad, if you like.

MARYLAND CRAB CAKES

SERVES
4

PREP *20 minutes plus chilling*
COOKING *10 minutes*

1 egg
2 tablespoons mayonnaise
2 teaspoons English mustard
dash of Worcestershire sauce
200g frozen brown crabmeat
4–6 tablespoons dried breadcrumbs
400g frozen or canned white crabmeat
4 spring onions, finely chopped
Old Bay seasoning (optional)
3–4 tablespoons any oil
cornflour or arrowroot powder, for dusting
salt and freshly ground black pepper
4 poached eggs, to serve (optional)

Canned and frozen crabmeat is really good quality. Here is an absolute classic, and if you can find Old Bay seasoning, then all the better. I have found it online and it adds a real classic twist to these lovely cakes.

1. Place the egg, mayo, mustard and Worcestershire sauce into a bowl. Add the brown crabmeat and breadcrumbs and mix well.

2. Next add the white crabmeat and spring onions and gently stir in. Try not to break up the meat too much. Season well with Old Bay seasoning, salt and pepper.

3. Mould into small patties and pop in the fridge for 1 hour to firm up.

4. Heat the oil in a frying pan over a medium heat. Remove the patties from the fridge, dust in a little cornflour or arrowroot powder and then, working in batches if needed, gently fry on each side for 3–4 minutes. Serve with poached eggs, if you like.

CHUNKY FISH FINGERS
& WAFFLES WITH SWEET & SOUR DIP

SERVES
4

PREP **15** *minutes*
COOKING **15–20** *minutes*

12 frozen fish fingers
4 frozen potato waffles, cooked
1 tablespoon any oil
200g frozen peas
200g frozen sweetcorn
100g baby spinach leaves

FOR THE DIP
8 tablespoons mayonnaise
1 tablespoon runny honey
1 tablespoon Worcestershire sauce
3 tablespoons tomato ketchup
finely grated zest and juice of 1 lime
1 tablespoon frozen chopped parsley
2 teaspoons Dijon mustard (optional)

One of my kids' favourites when they were growing up, this came about after a fridge and freezer raid at the end of a long day. Sometimes the best things come about by chance.

I. Bake or grill the fish fingers and waffles according to the packet instructions until nice and crisp.

2. Meanwhile, heat the oil in a small frying pan over a medium heat and cook the peas and sweetcorn for 4–5 minutes, stirring occasionally.

3. Place the mayo, honey, Worcestershire sauce, ketchup, lime zest and juice, parsley and mustard, if using, into a bowl and mix well.

4. Place a few spinach leaves on each plate with a warm waffle. Top with three fish fingers and surround with peas and a little sweetcorn.

5. Spoon over a little of the dip and serve the rest in a small bowl.

GRILLED PEPPERS WITH BLACK OLIVES

SERVES
4-6 as a side

PREP **10** *minutes*
COOKING **6-8** *minutes*

make ahead

VEGETARIAN
if using veggie Parmesan

2 large red peppers
2 large yellow peppers
2 green peppers
4 tablespoons olive oil
2 red onions, finely sliced
200g pitted black olives,
   roughly chopped
2-3 tablespoons extra virgin olive oil
juice of 1 lemon
3-4 tablespoons frozen chopped parsley
100g Parmesan cheese, grated
salt and freshly ground black pepper

Very simple and quick, this is an all-time favourite in our house. Even better, it can be cooked just before guests arrive and left warm until ready to serve.

I. Preheat a barbecue and leave until the coals are grey, or preheat a grill or oven to high.

2. Halve the peppers lengthways through the stalk and deseed (leave the stalk on).

3. Rub the peppers inside and out with the olive oil, season well and grill on each side for 3-4 minutes until soft and lightly coloured.

4. Meanwhile, place the onions, olives, extra virgin olive oil, lemon juice, parsley and cheese into a large serving bowl.

5. Add the hot, cooked peppers and toss well, then season again with salt and pepper.

PERFECT PASTA

EASY PEPPER & PASTA BROTH

SERVES
4

PREP **15** *minutes*
COOKING **20–25** *minutes*

vegan

150g spaghetti
400g can chopped tomatoes in juice
200ml passata
10g vegetable stock cube, crumbled
1kg frozen sliced peppers
vinegar, to taste
sugar, to taste
salt and freshly ground black pepper

TO SERVE
extra virgin olive oil, for drizzling
frozen baguette, baked and sliced

Frozen peppers are a really good ingredient to work with and are extremely good value. They save a lot of time, but you need to cook them in a broth or stew to get a deep flavour. If you decide to use them in other dishes, first roast them in a hot oven drizzled with a little oil to drive off the moisture. For a minestrone-style soup, use frozen mixed veg instead of peppers.

1. Place the spaghetti in a clean tea-towel and then break it up into small pieces using a rolling pin or by hand.

2. Place the tomatoes, passata, stock cube, peppers and 500ml water into a large saucepan. Bring to a simmer.

3. Add the broken spaghetti, mix well and then simmer gently for 15 minutes or until the spaghetti is cooked. You may need to add a little more water.

4. Season well with salt and pepper, then add vinegar and sugar to taste to balance all the flavours.

5. Serve in deep bowls with a swirl of extra virgin olive oil and baguette.

HALLOUMI, PASTA, HUMMUS & SUN-BLUSH TOMATO SALAD

SERVES
4

PREP **15** *minutes*
COOKING **10–15** *minutes*

make ahead

vegetarian

500g cooked macaroni pasta (approx. 260g dried weight), kept warm and oiled (see page 58, step 2)

150g good-quality hummus

200g sun-blush or sun-dried tomatoes, finely chopped

4 tablespoons frozen chopped basil

4 tablespoons frozen chopped parsley

2 tablespoons sherry vinegar

250g halloumi cheese, finely chopped

salt and freshly ground black pepper

crackers, rice cakes or breadsticks, to serve (optional)

A hearty dish that is packed full of flavour. Any cheese will suffice here, but halloumi works really well with the pasta, hummus and tomatoes. I sometimes add a few chopped fresh tomatoes and a few slices of spring onion, especially in the summertime.

1. Place the hummus, tomatoes, herbs and vinegar into a bowl and mix really well.

2. Next add the warm pasta and fold through. You may need to add a dash of water to let it out a little.

3. Finally add the cheese, salt and pepper, then lightly mix.

4. Serve with crackers, rice cakes or breadsticks.

BUTTERBEAN, PASTA & CHEESE PIE

SERVES
4

PREP **25 *minutes***
COOKING **30-35 *minutes***

vegan

200g frozen chopped onions

2 teaspoons dried garlic granules

500ml soya milk

4 tablespoons frozen chopped basil

10g vegetable stock cube, crumbled

2 tablespoons cornflour or arrowroot powder

200g vegan cheese, grated

260g orecchiette pasta, cooked (approx. 500g cooked weight)

2 × 400g cans butterbeans, well drained

200g breadcrumbs

salt and freshly ground black pepper

My absolute favourite, go-to, easy meal. It is vegan, but you can, as with most recipes, adapt it to your own preference. Add more or different beans or pulses if you like. I'm a huge fan of butterbeans, especially the large Greek ones you can buy in small cans in all the major supermarkets.

1. Preheat the grill to medium.

2. Place the onions, garlic granules, soya milk, basil and stock cube into a saucepan. Bring to a simmer, then cook for 5 minutes.

3. Mix the cornflour with a little water and stir into the simmering onion milk until it thickens.

4. Remove from the heat and season well with salt and pepper, then add 100g of the vegan cheese and whisk well.

5. Stir in the cooked orecchiette and beans, then spoon into an ovenproof baking dish and spread out evenly.

6. Sprinkle over the rest of the cheese and the breadcrumbs, then pop under the grill for 8–10 minutes to nicely brown.

TOMATO, RIGATONI & MOZZARELLA PASTA CAKE

SERVES
4-6

PREP **15** *minutes*
COOKING **45-50** *minutes*

make ahead

vegetarian

This dish is a bit of a showstopper, particularly when you cut into it. You can also make it using a bolognese sauce: swap the lentils for 350g beef mince and remove one can of tomatoes. I have also cooked this dish using larger cannelloni pasta and filling them with a mix of frozen spinach and ricotta cheese.

2 tablespoons olive oil, plus extra for greasing
1 small onion, very finely chopped
2 small celery sticks, very finely chopped
1 small carrot, very finely chopped
2 garlic cloves, finely chopped
pinch of dried oregano
2-3 tablespoons flour
1 tablespoon tomato purée
2 × 400g cans chopped tomatoes in juice
400g can green lentils
10g vegetable stock cube, crumbled
250g buffalo mozzarella, shredded
600g rigatoni pasta, blanched for 2 minutes
salt and freshly ground black pepper
handful of fresh basil and parsley, torn, to serve

1. Preheat the oven to 200°C/gas mark 6. Line and lightly oil a 25cm × 8cm-deep, loose-based cake tin.

2. Heat the olive oil in a pan over a medium heat. Add the onion, celery, carrot, garlic and oregano and cook for 3 minutes to soften.

3. Add the flour to soak up the juices and mix really well. Add the tomato purée, canned tomatoes, lentils, salt and pepper, then cook over a low heat for a few minutes.

4. Finally add the stock cube and 300ml water and bring to a very gentle simmer, then cook for 20 minutes until nice and thick.

5. Spoon half the tomato sauce and half the cheese into the bottom of the prepared cake tin. Carefully arrange the rigatoni, tightly packed together standing on their ends, in the tin. Spoon over the rest of the sauce and sprinkle over the rest of the cheese.

6. Bake in the oven for 15-20 minutes until cooked and golden, then remove and leave to cool for 15 minutes.

7. Sprinkle over the fresh basil and parsley. Remove the tin, slice and serve.

MEAT-FREE SPAGHETTI PIE

SERVES
4

PREP *25 minutes*
COOKING *45 minutes*

MAKE AHEAD
freeze after step 5

VEGETARIAN
if using veggie Parmesan

Bit of a twist on a lasagne by using spaghetti instead. It came about a few years ago when I had run out of lasagne sheets and had to feed the kids. It worked really well. In fact we called it spaghetti pie!

400g frozen green beans, roughly chopped
400g spaghetti
green salad, to serve (optional)

FOR THE SAUCE
2 tablespoons olive oil
2 small onions, finely chopped
4 garlic cloves, chopped
2 tablespoons plain flour
400g can chickpeas, drained
400g can borlotti beans, drained
400g can chopped tomatoes in juice
1 heaped tablespoon tomato purée
1 tablespoon dried oregano
10g vegetable stock cube, crumbled
salt and freshly ground black pepper

FOR THE WHITE SAUCE
600ml milk
40g soft butter
35g flour
75g Parmesan (or any) cheese,
    freshly grated
salt and freshly ground black pepper

1. Heat the oil in a pan over a medium heat and sauté the onions for 15 minutes. Add the garlic and cook for a further 2 minutes until golden. Add the flour and mix well to soak up the oil.

2. Mix in the chickpeas and borlotti beans. Add the tomatoes, tomato purée, oregano, stock cube, 100ml of water and salt and pepper. Bring to the boil and then simmer for 15 minutes, stirring occasionally to stop it catching.

3. Meanwhile for the white sauce, heat the milk to a simmer. Mix the butter and flour together well, then whisk into the simmering milk; it will thicken almost immediately. Add salt, pepper and half the cheese, then remove from the heat and keep warm.

4. Preheat the oven to 190°C/gas mark 5.

5. Stir the green beans into the tomato sauce, then spoon half into a 25cm square baking dish. Place over half the spaghetti and gently press in. Add a layer of white sauce, then a layer of bean sauce. Add the rest of the spaghetti and finally top with the rest of the white sauce.

6. Sprinkle over the rest of the cheese and bake in the oven for 35–40 minutes.

7. Remove from the oven and leave to slightly cool before eating with a large green salad.

BLUE CHEESE MACARONI WITH
HUMMUS & SUN-BLUSH TOMATOES

SERVES
4

PREP **15** *minutes*
COOKING **15** *minutes*

make ahead

VEGETARIAN
if using veggie cheese

150g good-quality hummus

200g sun-blush tomatoes, chopped

4 tablespoons frozen chopped basil

4 tablespoons frozen chopped parsley

2 tablespoons sherry vinegar

500g cooked macaroni pasta (approx. 260g dried weight), kept warm and oiled (see page 58, step 2)

200g blue cheese

salt and freshly ground black pepper

breadsticks or rice cakes, to serve

Nice mix of flavours and texture here. I use a mild blue cheese, but goats' cheese will also work. Just remember to leave the macaroni warm and oiled before you mix all the other ingredients.

1. Place the hummus, tomatoes, herbs and vinegar into a bowl and mix really well.

2. Add the warm pasta and fold through. You may need to add a dash of water to let it out a little.

3. Finally add the cheese, salt and pepper, then lightly mix. Serve with breadsticks or rice cakes.

MACARONI CHEESE

SERVES
2

PREP **15** *minutes*
COOKING **35** *minutes*

vegetarian

This brings back memories of learning to cook at my local technical college on day release from school. This was one of the first dishes I was ever taught, along with cottage pie and rough puff pastry. The base is still the same; the only thing I have added is a stock cube, and breadcrumbs on top as an optional extra.

200g dried macaroni
3 tablespoons olive oil
1 onion, very finely chopped
275ml milk
½ × 10g vegetable stock cube, crumbled
40g butter, softened
30g plain flour
175g strong Cheddar cheese, grated
1–2 pinches of ground nutmeg
1 tablespoon English mustard
4 tablespoons frozen chopped basil
4 slices of white bread, crusts removed and
    made into breadcrumbs
salt and freshly ground black pepper

1. Preheat the grill to hot, or preheat the oven to 190°C/gas mark 5.

2. Cook the macaroni in plenty of boiling water for 10 minutes until just cooked, then drain well and add a tablespoon of the oil to stop the pasta sticking together.

3. Warm the rest of the olive oil in a pan over a medium heat. Add the onion and fry for 5 minutes to soften. Add the milk and stock cube, then bring to the boil.

4. Meanwhile mix the butter and flour together to form a paste.

5. Once the milk is boiling, turn down the heat to a simmer, then whisk in the butter and flour mixture and cook for 2 minutes.

6. Take off the heat and stir in 125g of the cheese and the cooked macaroni. Add the nutmeg, mustard, salt and pepper and the chopped basil.

7. Spoon into an ovenproof dish, top with the rest of the grated Cheddar and the breadcrumbs, then brown under the grill or in the oven for about 10 minutes.

TUNA, SPINACH & SWEETCORN PASTA BAKE

SERVES
4-6

PREP **20** *minutes*
COOKING **45-50** *minutes*

MAKE AHEAD
freezable

This pasta dish has a really good texture as well as depth of flavour. Any canned fish works well, including mackerel, pilchards and sardines. It can be frozen and then reheated straight from the freezer. If you can't find anchovy essence, use canned anchovies: carefully crush three fillets to a paste with the flat of a heavy knife. Frozen sweetcorn, green beans, cauliflower and/or peas also work well in this dish.

250g fusilli pasta
30g butter
1 onion, finely chopped
2 heaped tablespoons plain flour
700ml milk
1 tablespoon anchovy essence
2 × 200g cans tuna in oil, drained well
150g frozen spinach, defrosted and drained well
    (squeeze to drain the liquid)
4 tablespoons frozen chopped basil
198g can sweetcorn, well drained (165g drained
    weight)
100g strong Cheddar, roughly grated
2-3 large beef tomatoes, sliced
salt and freshly ground black pepper
garlic bread, to serve (optional)

I. Preheat the oven to 200°C/gas mark 6.

2. Cook the pasta in plenty of salted boiling water according to the packet instructions, then drain really well.

3. Next, melt the butter in a pan over a medium heat. Add the onion and cook for 2–3 minutes, without colouring. Add the flour, stir to coat, then add the milk and whisk well. Bring to the boil whilst stirring; the sauce will nicely thicken.

4. Add the anchovy essence and some black pepper and mix well. Add the tuna, spinach, basil, sweetcorn and half the Cheddar. Mix really well.

5. Spoon into a large baking dish, then top with the beef tomatoes, overlapping them, and the rest of the cheese.

6. Bake in the oven for 25–30 minutes or until the cheese is nicely browned. Serve with garlic bread, if you like.

SARDINE, APPLE & FUSILLI SALAD

SERVES
4

PREP **15** *minutes*
COOKING **10–12** *minutes*

Yes, I know it sounds really odd, but it really does work well. I sometimes use half mayo and half soured cream for a less rich version. Any canned fish works in this recipe, including smoked oysters.

500g dried fusilli
2 × 250g cans sardines in oil, drained really well
2 small Pink Lady apples, cored and chopped
    into 5mm pieces (skin on)
finely grated zest and juice of 1 large lemon
100g frozen chopped onions
250ml soured cream
salt and freshly ground black pepper
breadsticks, to serve (optional)

1. Bring a large pan of water to the boil and add the pasta. Cook for 10–12 minutes or according to the packet instructions.

2. Drain, then place the pasta into a bowl and leave to come to room temperature.

3. In a bowl, break up the sardines into chunks; you do not want a mush. Set aside.

4. Place the apples in another bowl. Add the lemon juice and zest, and then mix well.

5. Add the frozen onions, salt, pepper and sardines, then gently mix together, ensuring you don't break up the chunks of fish.

6. Add the soured cream to the pasta and mix well, then finally fold through the fish and apple mix. Serve with breadsticks, if you like.

ONE POT

CHEAT'S CHICKEN TIKKA MASALA

SERVES
4

PREP **40** *minutes*
COOKING **30-40** *minutes*

Not very authentic, I know, but nevertheless extremely tasty. I was always told that the original recipe in Glasgow used a can of tomato soup as the base, as I do here.

FOR THE CHICKEN
finely grated zest and juice of 1 large lemon
finely grated zest and juice of 1 lime
6 tablespoons thick yogurt
4 chicken breasts, skin on,
    cut into 4cm cubes
4 tablespoons vegetable oil
salt and freshly ground black pepper

FOR THE SAUCE
4 tablespoons vegetable oil
1 tablespoon ground coriander
2 teaspoons ground turmeric
2 teaspoons paprika
2 tablespoons grated ginger
1 teaspoon garam masala
1 small red chilli, very finely chopped
½ teaspoon ground cloves
2 onions, very finely chopped
4 garlic cloves, chopped
400g can tomato soup
10g chicken stock cube, crumbled
125ml whipping cream
sugar, to taste
2 tablespoons cold unsalted butter, cubed
coriander leaves, to serve

1. Place the lemon and lime zests and juices into a bowl with the yogurt and mix really well. Add the chicken pieces and mix well again with a little salt and pepper. Cover and leave to marinate in the fridge for 15–20 minutes.

2. For the sauce, heat the oil in a saucepan over a medium heat. Add the spices and fry for 1–2 minutes. Add the onions and garlic and cook for 2–3 minutes. Add the tomato soup, stock cube, cream and a little water and simmer for 15–20 minutes or until the onions are cooked and the sauce has slightly reduced.

3. Blitz the sauce in a blender or with a handheld blender until very smooth. Pour back into the saucepan and bring to the boil.

4. Remove the chicken from the fridge. Heat the oil in a frying pan over a medium heat and gently sauté the chicken for 2–3 minutes until a little coloured.

5. Place straight into the simmering sauce and simmer for 6–10 minutes to finish cooking; do not overcook. Season well with salt, pepper and sugar to balance.

6. Finally add the butter and shake the pan until the sauce has thickened and is glossy. Serve with a few coriander leaves on top.

CORNED BEEF HASH

SERVES
2

PREP **10** *minutes*
COOKING **35** *minutes*

One of my favourite go-to, quick meals – it hits all the spots! If you prefer, you can use canned new potatoes instead of frozen roasties. They work equally well. This is particularly good served with a fried egg and pickled red cabbage.

3 tablespoons vegetable oil
250g frozen chopped onions
450g frozen roasted potatoes, roughly chopped
10g beef stock cube, crumbled
2 tablespoons Worcestershire sauce
340g can corned beef, cut into 2cm chunks
salt and freshly ground black pepper

TO SERVE (OPTIONAL)
fried eggs
pickled red cabbage

I. Heat the vegetable oil in a large saucepan with a lid over a medium heat.

2. Add the onions and cook for 10 minutes until lightly coloured. If you've taken the onions straight from the freezer, you will need to cook them for longer to evaporate any water as they defrost. Don't worry, just increase the heat to high and leave them for a few minutes until they start to brown.

3. Add the potatoes and cook over a high heat, stirring everything together, for 10 minutes.

4. Add 100ml cold water, the stock cube, the Worcestershire sauce, salt and pepper, and cook, stirring occasionally, for a few minutes until nearly all the liquid has evaporated.

5. Add the corned beef, then stir well. Reduce the heat to low, cover and then leave for 10 minutes to just warm through. Serve with a fried egg and pickled cabbage, if you like.

ROASTED CAULIFLOWER & POTATO TORTILLA

SERVES
4

PREP **15** *minutes*
COOKING **40-45** *minutes*

vegetarian

I have to be honest, until last year I wouldn't have even noticed canned potatoes in the supermarket, let alone bought or cooked with them. But as the shelves started to be cleared of all the more popular cans such as sweetcorn, tomatoes and baked beans, others became more visible. I did buy canned spuds with some trepidation, but I have to say I was pleasantly surprised. In certain dishes like this, or a light potato and spinach curry, they work very well indeed. Go on, try it.

4 tablespoons olive oil
2 onions, finely chopped
1 small cauliflower, broken into small florets
5 large eggs
10 cherry tomatoes, halved
560g can potatoes, drained (345g drained
    weight), then peeled and cut into small cubes
salt and freshly ground black pepper

1. Preheat the oven to 200°C/gas mark 6.

2. Heat the oil in a large, ovenproof, non-stick frying pan over a medium heat. Add the onions and cauliflower and cook for 10 minutes to soften.

3. Pop into the oven and cook for 15–20 minutes until the cauli has a good colour and is cooked through, then leave to slightly cool.

4. Break the eggs into a bowl, season with salt and pepper, then break up a little with a fork.

5. Spread the tomatoes over the cooked cauliflower along with the potatoes.

6. Pour over the eggs, then shake the pan gently to evenly combine the ingredients.

7. Place the pan over a low heat for a few minutes until the eggs begin to set at the bottom and the sides.

8. Place the pan in the oven and cook for about 10 minutes, then remove and leave to cool for 10 minutes.

9. Carefully invert onto a large dinner plate. Serve hot, warm or cold.

CRISPY HASH POTATOES
WITH BACON & ONIONS

SERVES
4

PREP **20** *minutes*
COOKING **30-40** *minutes*

I have made this dish using frozen baked potatoes and frozen roasted potatoes and both work. Either way, it's a very easy, tasty dish, so the choice is up to you. You can also substitute a small can of corned beef, chopped, instead of the bacon.

3 tablespoons olive oil
300g smoked, rindless, thick bacon pieces
2 small onions, finely chopped
4 large frozen baked or roasted potatoes (or fresh and cooked), roughly chopped
2 teaspoons celery salt
2 pinches of crumbled chicken stock cube
freshly ground black pepper

1. Preheat the oven to 200°C/gas mark 6.

2. Place the oil, bacon and onions into a large, ovenproof, non-stick frying pan over a medium heat. Fry for 10 minutes to soften.

3. Add the cooked potatoes to the onions and bacon. Stir well, then pop into the oven for 20-30 minutes until just coloured and cooked through.

4. Remove from the oven and season well with the celery salt, stock cube and pepper. Stir well, then serve.

BROAD BEAN, RED PESTO
& CHEDDAR FRITTATA

SERVES
4–6

PREP *20 minutes*
COOKING *30–35 minutes*

make ahead

VEGETARIAN
if using veggie pesto

I simply love frozen baby broad beans. They are so good, I'm astounded that more chefs don't use them. Here I combine them with microwaveable quinoa and pop in a frittata. Red pesto brings everything together and gives the dish a lovely colour. A great light lunch dish.

4 tablespoons olive oil
200g frozen chopped onions
250g packet microwaveable quinoa
500g frozen baby broad beans, defrosted
6 golden-yolk eggs
200ml milk
150g jar red pesto
100g Cheddar cheese, grated
salt and freshly ground black pepper

1. Preheat the oven to 200°C/gas mark 6.

2. Heat a large, ovenproof, non-stick frying pan over a medium heat. Add the oil and onions and cook for 10 minutes.

3. Microwave the quinoa and add to the pan with the broad beans.

4. In a bowl, whisk the eggs, milk and pesto really well with salt and pepper. Pour this over the bean quinoa and shake the pan to remove any trapped air.

5. Evenly sprinkle over the cheese, then pop into the oven and cook for 15 minutes or until just set.

6. Remove from the oven and leave to rest for 15 minutes. Cut into wedges and serve.

CABBAGE, ONION & CANNELLINI BEAN STEW

SERVES
4

PREP **10** *minutes*
COOKING **20** *minutes*

VEGETARIAN/VEGAN
if using veggie/vegan pesto

250g frozen chopped onions
2 × 10g vegetable stock cubes, crumbled
2–3 tablespoons green pesto
1 small white cabbage, cut into thin wedges
2 × 400g cans cannellini beans, drained
200g frozen peas
200g frozen green beans
4 tablespoons extra virgin olive oil
salt and freshly ground black pepper

I like cabbage in any form but especially when it's gently cooked with beans, green vegetables, pesto and lots of olive oil. This dish is deceptively simple but is packed with flavour and colour.

1. Place the onions, stock cubes, pesto and cabbage in a saucepan with 1 litre of water. Bring to a simmer and cook for 10 minutes.

2. Add the beans, peas and green beans and simmer for 5 minutes; do not overcook.

3. Season well with pepper: you may not need salt as you have stock cubes and pesto already. Add the extra virgin olive oil, swirl through and serve.

SWEET POTATO, CAULIFLOWER & PEANUT CURRY

SERVES
4

PREP **15 minutes**
COOKING **30-35 minutes**

vegan

An easy curry that uses ingredients straight from the freezer with no need to defrost. The depth of flavour comes from using a stock cube and peanut butter as the base.

4 tablespoons any oil
250g frozen chopped onions
1 tablespoon dried garlic granules
½ teaspoon dried chilli flakes
2 tablespoons frozen chopped ginger
400g can coconut milk
2 heaped tablespoons peanut butter
10g vegetable stock cube, crumbled
500g frozen cubed sweet potato
500g frozen cauliflower florets
1–2 tablespoons cornflour
300g (about 6 × 50g balls) frozen spinach
1–2 teaspoons sugar
salt and freshly ground black pepper
2 × 250g packets microwaveable basmati rice, warmed, to serve

1. Heat the oil in a pan over a high heat and then add the onions, garlic granules, chilli flakes and ginger. Cook for 6–8 minutes to drive off the moisture and colour a little.

2. Add the coconut milk, half-fill the can with water, then add to the pan along with the peanut butter and stock cube and whisk. Bring to a simmer, then cook for 5 minutes.

3. Add the frozen sweet potato and cauliflower and bring back to a simmer for 10 minutes.

4. Mix the cornflour well with 2 tablespoons of cold water and then add to the simmering curry: it will thicken pretty much straight away.

5. Check the seasoning and adjust if needed, then drop in the frozen spinach pucks. Cover and simmer for 5 minutes, then stir in the sugar, turn off the heat and leave for 15 minutes.

6. Stir well and serve with the basmati rice.

THE VEGETABLE AS KING

ROASTED CAULIFLOWER WITH SALSA VERDE

SERVES
4–6

PREP **40** *minutes*
COOKING **20** *minutes*

For many years I wasn't really a fan of frozen cauliflower, but I have discovered it has really improved. Once defrosted and drained well, it doesn't leach much water. Like a lot of frozen veg, it needs a bit of help to release the flavour, so I roast it in a hot oven. Don't be frightened to overcook it slightly. The only fresh ingredient here is the boiled eggs, though you can buy them ready boiled!

FOR THE CAULIFLOWER
1kg frozen cauliflower florets, defrosted and
    well drained
2 tablespoons any oil
salt and freshly ground black pepper

FOR THE SALSA VERDE
8 tablespoons frozen chopped parsley
8 tablespoons frozen chopped basil
2 teaspoons dried garlic granules
2 tablespoons chopped capers
2 tablespoons chopped gherkins
4 canned salted anchovy fillets, chopped
2 teaspoons white wine vinegar
2 teaspoons tarragon Dijon mustard
pinch of dried chilli flakes
200ml extra virgin olive oil
yolk of 2 hard-boiled eggs, passed through
    a sieve

1. Preheat the oven to 220°C/gas mark 7.

2. Place the drained cauliflower onto a baking tray and season really well with salt and pepper. Add the oil and mix really well, then roast in the oven for 20 minutes until nicely coloured.

3. Remove from the oven and leave to come to room temperature.

4. Meanwhile, place all the salsa verde ingredients except for the eggs and olive oil into a food-processor and blitz until you have a chunky purée.

5. Gradually add the oil in a thin stream as you mix: you may need a little more depending on your taste. Add a dash of water if needed, then finally add the egg. Set aside for 30 minutes to infuse.

6. Spoon the salsa verde into a bowl and mix well, then check the seasoning. Add the warm roasted cauliflower and mix really well. Serve.

RUSSIAN SALAD

SERVES
4

PREP **10** *minutes*
COOKING **30** *minutes*

vegan

1.5kg mixed frozen vegetables

4 tablespoons olive oil

300ml egg-free mayonnaise (shop-bought or homemade, see page 120)

fresh or frozen herbs such as basil, parsley or chives, to taste (optional)

salt and freshly ground black pepper

This salad was very popular when I was training to be a chef. It has made a bit of a comeback over the past couple of years, and I rather like it. Here I use an eggless mayo instead of the normal version. I use two bags of frozen peas, beans, carrots and sweetcorn and to intensify the flavour even more, I roast them before adding the mayo. It can be a meal on its own or serve with boiled eggs, grilled chicken or even some crispy bacon.

1. Preheat the oven to 220°C/gas mark 7.

2. Spread the vegetables evenly over a baking tray. Drizzle over the olive oil and season really well with salt and pepper. Mix well.

3. Place in the oven and cook for 15 minutes.

4. Stir well and then cook for a further 15 minutes. Remove from the oven and leave to cool.

5. Add the mayonnaise and green herbs, if you like, then mix well. Serve.

SPICY BUTTERBEANS WITH
CRISPY GARLIC & TOASTED ALMONDS

SERVES
4

PREP **15** *minutes*
COOKING **20** *minutes*

vegan

4 tablespoons olive oil
2 small onions, very finely chopped
2 garlic cloves, finely chopped
400g can butterbeans, well drained
400g can chopped tomatoes in juice
1 tablespoon tomato purée
pinch of dried chilli flakes
2 tablespoons any vinegar
10g vegetable stock cube, crumbled
4 ripe tomatoes, chopped

FOR THE TOPPING
2 tablespoons any oil
6–8 garlic cloves, finely sliced
pinch of salt
pinch of pepper
pinch of sugar
100g flaked almonds, lightly toasted

Perfect served with a green salad and crunchy baguette.

1. Heat the olive oil in a pan over a medium heat, add the onions and the chopped garlic and soften for 2 minutes.

2. Add the beans, canned tomatoes, tomato purée, chilli flakes, vinegar and stock cube. Bring to a simmer and cook for 10 minutes, or until the onions are soft and the mixture has thickened.

3. Remove from the heat and stir in the fresh tomatoes.

4. For the topping, heat the oil in a frying pan over a medium heat. Add the sliced garlic and then cook until really coloured and crispy but not burnt. Season well with salt, pepper and a little sugar.

5. Spoon the beans into bowls and top with the toasted almonds and crisp garlic shards.

ASPARAGUS QUICHE

SERVES
4

PREP **30** *minutes*
COOKING **1** *hour*

make ahead

vegetarian

Now I know exactly what you are all thinking: canned asparagus ... yuk. Well let me tell you, when I was a kid, it was the only asparagus I ever saw or tasted. Quite ironically the flavour profile of canned asparagus – or even asparagus soup mix – is still used to this day as a basis for most asparagus-flavoured products. It tastes pretty much nothing like fresh, grilled asparagus spears, but it works as an almost separate flavour for certain dishes.

FOR THE BASE
500g frozen shortcrust pastry, defrosted
1 egg white, beaten

FOR THE FILLING
3–4 tablespoons olive oil
250g frozen chopped onions
425g can asparagus spears,
    well drained, then halved
2 eggs
1 egg yolk
400ml milk
1 teaspoon ground coriander
100g Gruyère cheese
salt and freshly ground black pepper

1. Preheat the oven to 180°C/gas mark 4.

2. Roll out the pastry nice and thin, then use to line a 36 × 12 × 3cm-deep, rectangular, loose-based flan tin: make sure you have a nice high lip above the edge of the tin. Dock with a fork, then chill well.

3. Line the flan with greaseproof paper and fill with baking beans. Bake for 15 minutes to just set. Remove the beans and paper, being very careful not to damage the pastry.

4. Brush with the beaten egg white and return to the oven for 5 minutes to seal the pastry.

5. Heat the olive oil in a frying pan over a high heat. Add the onions and fry for 10 minutes to slightly soften. Spoon into the base of the flan tin, then place the asparagus neatly on top.

6. Whisk the eggs, yolk and milk together and season with salt, pepper and ground coriander.

7. Place the flan tin on a baking tray and then place in the oven. Carefully pour in the custard until the flan is really full. Bake for 30–35 minutes until just set, then remove and leave to cool to room temperature.

8. Cut the flan into four and finely grate over the cheese just before serving.

BRUSSELS SPROUT BUBBLE TRAY BAKE

SERVES
4

PREP **20** *minutes*
COOKING **20-30** *minutes*

vegetarian

400g frozen mash, defrosted
200g canned or frozen chestnuts,
　　roughly chopped
200g frozen roastedpotatoes, roughly chopped
8 spring onions, finely chopped
200g frozen Brussel sprouts, cooked and
　　roughly chopped
1 egg
olive oil, for drizzling
salt and freshly ground black pepper

Incredibly easy and straight to the point. In fact, any frozen vegetables work really well in this tray bake. I also sometimes add a can of borlotti beans to bulk it out. Top with fried or poached eggs and a nice dollop of pesto or mayo, if you like.

1. Preheat the oven to 200°C/gas mark 6 and line a large baking tray with greaseproof paper.

2. Roughly mix together all the ingredients, pack into the baking tray and drizzle with a little olive oil.

3. Bake in the oven for 20–30 minutes until well coloured.

SMOKED TOFU & CHILLI NOODLES

SERVES
4

PREP **15** *minutes*
COOKING **10** *minutes*

vegan

200g (4 nests) dried instant rice noodles
4 tablespoons olive oil
200g frozen chopped onions
1 teaspoon dried garlic granules
¼ teaspoon dried chilli flakes
250g firm smoked tofu, cubed
3–4 tablespoons dark soy sauce, plus extra
to serve
3 tablespoons roasted peanuts, crushed
½ small cucumber, finely chopped
4 tablespoons frozen chopped coriander

I rather like smoked tofu. I always feel it's doing me some good whilst at the same time being hearty and filling. I think you do need to add some bold strong flavours and textures, though, to help it along the way. This nice, simple recipe is one I had in Vietnam a few years ago and have never forgotten.

1. Place the noodles in a large bowl, cover with boiling salted water and leave for 10 minutes to soften and swell.

2. Meanwhile, heat the oil in a pan over a high heat. Add the onions, garlic granules and chilli flakes, and then sauté for 2–3 minutes.

3. Add the tofu and stir to warm through for 2–3 minutes.

4. Reduce the heat to medium, then stir in the softened noodles and soy sauce. Cook for 3–4 minutes.

5. Remove from the heat and stir through the peanuts, cucumber and coriander. Serve straight away with a dash more soy sauce.

SPICED 5 CAN DAL WITH GINGER & ONIONS

SERVES
4

PREP **15** *minutes*
COOKING **20** *minutes*

make ahead

vegetarian

400g can green lentils, drained and rinsed

400g can chickpeas, drained and rinsed

2 × 10g vegetable stock cubes, crumbled

2 garlic cloves, chopped

400g can cannellini beans, drained and rinsed

400g can borlotti beans, drained and rinsed

400g can kidney beans, drained and rinsed

4 tablespoons vegetable oil

50g piece of fresh ginger, peeled and finely
   sliced (about 2 tablespoons)

1 tablespoon finely sliced red or green chilli
   (about 1 chilli)

2 onions, finely sliced

½ teaspoon ground cumin

1 teaspoon turmeric

salt and freshly ground black pepper

TO SERVE

4–6 tablespoons thick yogurt

a few sprigs of fresh coriander

4 soft flour tortillas

There is something really satisfying about
a deep, thick stew of pulses. Not only is it
really good for you, but also it is really easy
to prepare and cook. This dish is a classic
example of a hearty dish without meat or fish.

I. Place the lentils, chickpeas, stock cubes and
garlic into a food-processor with about 350ml
cold water, and then blitz to a smooth paste.

2. Pour into a saucepan and then add the
cannellini, borlotti and kidney beans. Stir well
and bring to a simmer. Cook for 15 minutes
until nice and thick.

3. Meanwhile heat the oil in a large frying pan
over a high heat. Add the ginger and chilli,
then cook for 3–4 minutes until really nicely
coloured. Add the onions and spices, season
and then continue to cook for a further 5–6
minutes until the onions are well coloured.

4. To serve spoon the thick stew into small,
deep bowls, top with the spiced onion mix, a
blob of yogurt, fresh coriander and soft tortillas.

FRIED TOFU
WITH GINGER DIPPING SAUCE

SERVES
4

PREP **25** *minutes*
COOKING **10–15** *minutes*

vegetarian

FOR THE TOFU

vegetable oil, for deep-frying

½ egg white

3 tablespoons cornflour

pinch of salt

½ teaspoon five-spice powder

½ teaspoon sesame oil

500g firm tofu, cut into 2cm cubes, then patted
   dry on kitchen paper

FOR THE DIP

6 tablespoons dark soy sauce

2 tablespoons white wine vinegar

2 teaspoons sesame oil

2 tablespoons frozen chopped ginger

4 tablespoons frozen chopped coriander

1 teaspoon sugar

Another really easy dish to make and cook
and, when coupled with the dipping sauce,
a really tasty meal, too. I sometimes serve it
with stir-fried pak choi or baby spinach leaves
and a few fresh beansprouts.

I. In a bowl, mix all the ingredients for the
dipping sauce together well.

2. Heat a large wok or deep frying pan with
2–3cm of vegetable oil to roughly 180°C.

3. Place the egg white, 1 tablespoon of the
cornflour and the salt, five spice and sesame oil
into a bowl and whisk well.

4. Dust the tofu in the rest of the cornflour, then
pop into the egg white mix and coat really well.

5. Working in batches, deep fry for 4–5 minutes,
or until golden and crisp, then drain on kitchen
paper. Serve warm with the dipping sauce.

GREEN VEGETABLE MASSAMAN CURRY

SERVES
4

PREP *25 minutes*
COOKING *25 minutes*

MAKE VEGAN
omit fish sauce

2 tablespoons any oil

200g frozen chopped onions

4 garlic cloves, finely chopped

1–2 tablespoons green massaman curry paste

400g can coconut milk

10g vegetable stock cube, crumbled

560g can potatoes, drained (345g drained weight), then chopped into walnut-sized chunks

1 teaspoon palm or light brown sugar

juice of 2 limes

1 teaspoon fish sauce, or to taste (optional)

2–3 tablespoons tamarind paste

dash of light soy sauce

100ml pineapple juice (optional)

200g frozen peas

200g frozen green beans, cut into 2cm pieces

2 tablespoons roasted peanuts, toasted and chopped

salt

TO SERVE

2 tablespoons Thai basil, shredded

Jasmine or sticky rice

1 lime, cut into wedges

An easy recipe that tastes really good and is really adaptable; add as many different ingredients as you like to enhance the base. Try adding prawns, cooked chicken or even roasted vegetables such as pumpkin, squash and courgettes. If you can, cut the potato using a serrated cutter.

1. Heat the oil in a pan over a medium heat. Add the onions and garlic and fry for 3–4 minutes until nicely golden.

2. Add the curry paste and stir through, then add the coconut milk, stock cube and 150ml of water. Bring to the boil.

3. Add the potatoes, sugar, lime juice, fish sauce, if using, tamarind, soy sauce and pineapple juice, if using, and then simmer for 10 minutes.

4. Taste, then season with a little salt: be careful as a lot of pre-made pastes are highly seasoned. Add the peas, beans and peanuts and warm through.

5. Serve with the shredded Thai basil, Jasmine or sticky rice and wedges of lime.

FISH FAVOURITES

ULTIMATE FISH FINGER WRAP

SERVES
4

PREP **15 minutes**
COOKING **10 minutes**

MAKE AHEAD
refrigerate after step 3

Who doesn't love a fish finger? Here is a wrap version that works pretty much as a main meal. The secret is to get the fish fingers nice and crunchy; if you can deep-fry them, all the better. I serve with onion rings.

2 tablespoons vegetable oil
8 chunky fish fingers
4 × 24cm soft flour tortilla wraps
¼ Iceberg lettuce, cut into large pieces
4 slices of smoked streaky bacon,
    grilled or fried until crispy
2 hard-boiled eggs (about 6 minutes), halved
4 tablespoons mayonnaise
fresh basil leaves
2 spring onions, finely sliced
1 carrot, finely grated (optional)
salt and freshly ground black pepper
onion rings, to serve (see opposite)

1. Heat the oil in a pan over a medium heat and fry the fish fingers for 4–5 minutes on each side until crunchy. Alternatively, grill under a medium heat.

2. Lay out a wrap on a chopping board. Place a little Iceberg lettuce down one end of the wrap. Top with one slice of bacon, sprinkle with a little salt and pepper, then add two fish fingers. Add half a boiled egg, 1 tablespoon of the mayo, a few basil leaves, a sprinkling of spring onions and some of the carrot, if you want.

3. Fold the bottom edge over, then fold in both sides and roll up tight. Wrap tightly with clingfilm, then chill well in the fridge.

4. Remove the clingfilm and halve diagonally. Serve with onion rings, if you like.

THE BEST ONION RINGS

SERVES
4

PREP **15** *minutes*
COOKING **5–10** *minutes*

vegan

sunflower oil, for deep-frying
150g self-raising flour, plus extra for dusting
250ml sparkling water
2 onions, sliced into 5mm rings

I. Preheat a deep-fat fryer or fill a deep pan one third full with oil and heat to 190°C. If you don't have a thermometer, test the oil is hot enough by adding a small cube of bread; it should brown in 40 seconds.

2. Place the flour in a bowl, then whisk in enough of the water to have a thickish batter.

3. Dust the onion rings in a little flour, then place into the batter. Gently shake off any excess and then deep-fry for 4–5 minutes until crisp and golden brown. Drain on kitchen paper.

EASY FISH TACOS

SERVES
4

PREP **20** *minutes*
COOKING **10** *minutes*

4 tablespoons any oil

8 spring onions, thinly sliced on the diagonal

1 garlic cloves, finely chopped

400g can cannellini beans, well drained

198g can sweetcorn, well drained (165g drained weight)

200g mayonnaise

125g can mackerel, well drained

418g can salmon, well drained

squeeze of lemon juice

8 soft or crunchy tacos

2 heads Little Gem lettuce or similar hard lettuce such as Romaine or Cos, shredded

4 tablespoons chopped fresh or frozen coriander (about 1 small bunch if fresh)

2 tablespoons Sriracha or sweet chilli sauce (optional)

Canned fish in all its forms is pretty good and extremely good value for money. I even recently bought Alaskan king crab in a can; it was good but wasn't cheap! These tacos are one of my recent favourites and make for a great light lunch.

1. Heat the oil in a pan over a medium heat. Add the spring onions and garlic, and then soften for 5 minutes. Add the beans and warm through for 2 minutes.

2. Spoon the contents of the pan into a bowl and gently break down with a fork or potato masher: don't go mad. Add the sweetcorn, mix well and leave to cool.

3. Next add the mayo and mix well again.

4. Gently flake the fish into nice pieces – not too small – and add to the bowl along with the lemon juice. Carefully fold together.

5. Lay out a soft tortilla or position the crisp versions and place a little lettuce into each one. Evenly spoon in the fish mix, then top with a little coriander and spicy sauce. Either fold or serve as is.

MIXED FISH BAKE WITH WAFFLE TOPPING

SERVES
4

PREP **15** *minutes*
COOKING **50-55** *minutes*

Another great example of how a familiar frozen product can be used to make a simple meal with real flavour. I came up with the topping when my kids were little and I'd forgotten to buy potatoes to go on their fish pie. I looked in the freezer and hey ho! Frozen hash browns also work really well as a topping.

1kg frozen mixed seafood

150g frozen green beans

150g frozen peas

2 tablespoons frozen chopped parsley

2 tablespoons frozen chopped tarragon

700ml milk

200g frozen chopped onions

10g fish stock cube, crumbled

65g plain four

75g salted butter, well softened

2 teaspoons fish sauce (optional)

10 frozen potato waffles, defrosted
    and cut into squares

salt and freshly ground black pepper

tomato ketchup or mayonnaise, to serve
    (optional)

I. Preheat the oven to 200°C/gas mark 6.

2. Place the frozen seafood, beans, peas and herbs into a large bowl and set aside.

3. Place the milk, onions, stock cube, salt and pepper into a thick-based saucepan and bring to a simmer. Cook for 5 minutes to soften the onions.

4. In another bowl, mix the flour, butter and fish sauce, if using, to a smooth paste. Whisk in the milk and onion mix; the sauce will quickly thicken.

5. Pour over the frozen seafood and mix really well, then spoon into a deep baking dish (ideally deep enough for the mix to fill three quarters).

6. Place the waffle squares on top in a diagonal pattern, then pop into the oven and cook for 40-45 minutes or until the centre of the pie is piping hot.

7. Remove from the oven and leave to cool for 20 minutes. Serve with a dash of tomato ketchup or a spoon of mayo.

FRESH (FROZEN) TUNA BURGERS

SERVES
4

PREP **15** *minutes plus chilling*
COOKING **8-10** *minutes*

I'm a real convert to frozen tuna. Along with fish like salmon, it freezes and defrosts very well. Pretty much all frozen tuna steaks are vacuum packed, which means they keep extremely well. You just need to remember to remove the steaks from the vacuum packs and dry them with kitchen paper before cracking on with the recipe.

350–450g frozen yellowfin tuna, defrosted
1–2 tablespoons mayonnaise, plus extra to serve
1 tablespoon freshly grated ginger
finely grated zest of 1 small lemon
1 egg, beaten
100g panko breadcrumbs
2 tablespoons olive oil
salt and freshly ground black pepper
Tomato & Red Onion Salad (see opposite),
    to serve

1. Open the packs of tuna and dry really well on kitchen paper. Chop the tuna really finely, then chill well.

2. Mix the chilled tuna with the mayo, ginger and lemon zest and juice, and then season well with salt and pepper.

3. Mould into four even, plump patties, then slightly press. Brush each side of the four patties with the beaten egg and dust with a few breadcrumbs.

4. Heat the olive oil in a pan over a medium heat. Add the patties and cook for 4–5 minutes on each side, ensuring you keep the tuna nice and rare. Serve warm with the tomato salad and a spoon of mayo.

TOMATO & RED ONION SALAD

SERVES
4

PREP **20** *minutes*
COOKING *none*

vegan

4 large, ripe plum or vine tomatoes,
   at room temperature
5 red spring onions, very finely sliced
   on the diagonal
50g fresh rocket (optional)

FOR THE DRESSING
2 tablespoons any vinegar
   (I love sherry vinegar)
1 heaped teaspoon Dijon mustard
pinch of sugar
4 tablespoons sunflower oil
1 tablespoon extra virgin olive oil (optional)
salt and freshly ground black pepper

I. Make the dressing by placing the vinegar, mustard and a pinch each of salt, pepper and sugar into a bowl. Whisk in the oil(s) and adjust the seasoning if needed.

2. Slice the tomatoes horizontally, not too thinly. Layer the tomato slices with the red spring onion slices and rocket, if using.

3. Spoon over the dressing and leave to rest for 15 minutes before serving.

TUNA, NOODLE & SWEETCORN CAKES
WITH DIPPING SAUCE

SERVES
4

PREP **10** *minutes*
COOKING **15-20** *minutes*

A light, tasty dish that is really easy to prepare and cook. Any canned fish or even meat will work in this recipe. The great thing about tuna though, is that a little goes a long way in the flavour stakes, so using two small cans really does the job; even one can will do, at a push.

FOR THE SWEETCORN CAKES
100g (2 nests) dried instant rice noodles
4 tablespoons any oil
2 onions
198g can sweetcorn, drained (165g drained weight)
2 × 145g cans tuna in brine, well drained
2 eggs
2–3 tablespoons self-raising or plain flour
2–3 tablespoons mayonnaise
salt and freshly ground black pepper

FOR THE DIPPING SAUCE
2 tablespoons soy sauce
1 tablespoon sesame oil
2 tablespoons finely chopped fresh ginger
4 tablespoons chopped frozen coriander
pinch of sugar
dash of vinegar

1. Place the rice noodles in a large bowl and cover with boiling water, then leave for 10 minutes.

2. Meanwhile, heat 2 tablespoons of the oil in a pan over a high heat. Add the onions and sweetcorn and cook for 10 minutes to soften and colour.

3. Place the tuna into a bowl along with the eggs, flour and mayonnaise, then add the onions and sweetcorn.

4. Drain the noodles well and roughly chop with a knife. Add to the sweetcorn and tuna, then mix well. Season with salt and pepper.

5. Make up the dipping sauce by mixing all the ingredients together in a bowl.

6. Heat a large frying pan over a medium heat and add the rest of the oil. Spoon large dollops of the noodle mix, spread slightly and cook for 3–4 minutes, then flip over and cook for a further 4–5 minutes. Lift out and keep warm while you repeat with the rest of the mixture.

7. Serve warm with the dipping sauce.

BRUNCH SALMON HASH

SERVES
4

PREP **25** *minutes*
COOKING **15-20** *minutes*

make ahead

Canned fish has been a staple for me ever since I was fed canned sardines, pilchards in tomato sauce and canned salmon sandwiches, which my grandmother loved on a Sunday evening. Here is a twist on a fishcake but adding lots of flavour from storecupboard ingredients to stretch a 400g can a little bit further. It's a perfect example of how convenience cooking can be really tasty.

FOR THE HASH CAKES
400g can salmon
1 egg
1 tablespoon cornflour
1 tablespoon Dijon mustard
finely grated zest and juice of 1 small lemon
2–3 tablespoons olive oil
4 tablespoons flour, for dusting

FOR THE TOMATO SAUCE
400g can chopped tomatoes in juice
198g can sweetcorn, drained (165g drained weight)
4 tablespoons balsamic vinegar
½ × 10g vegetable stock cube, crumbled

FOR THE MAYONNAISE
4 tablespoons mayonnaise
6 tablespoons roughly chopped fresh dill (optional)
2 teaspoons Dijon mustard
salt and freshly ground black pepper

I. Gently break up the salmon with a fork. Place in a bowl and add the egg, cornflour, mustard and lemon zest and juice, then bring together. Mould into four patties and slightly flatten, then chill in the fridge for 20 minutes.

2. Place the chopped tomatoes, sweetcorn and vinegar into a saucepan along with the stock cube. Cook over a medium heat for 5–6 minutes to slightly thicken, then keep warm.

3. Heat a non-stick frying pan over a low heat and add the olive oil. Dust the hash cakes with the flour and cook in the pan for 3–4 minutes on each side; do not overcook.

4. In a small bowl, mix the mayonnaise with the dill, mustard and pepper.

5. Spoon the tomato sauce onto four plates and place the hash cakes on top with a nice spoon of the mayo and dill.

REALLY EASY SALMON
WITH HERB MAYO

SERVES
4

PREP **10** *minutes*
COOKING **10-15** *minutes*

This simple recipe uses frozen salmon plus a few other storecupboard ingredients to make a nice dish that's not only colourful but also really delicious. Most frozen fish fillets such as haddock, cod loins, basa and wild salmon work well in this recipe. Just remember to dry the fish well with kitchen paper and do not overcook.

4 × 200g frozen salmon fillets, skin on,
    defrosted and patted dry with kitchen paper
2 tablespoons any oil

FOR THE RUB
1 tablespoon dried garlic granules
1 teaspoon salt
½ teaspoon freshly ground black pepper
1 teaspoon soft brown sugar
1 teaspoon ground cumin
1 teaspoon smoked paprika

FOR THE MAYO
8–10 tablespoons mayonnaise
2 heaped tablespoons frozen chopped coriander
2 heaped tablespoons frozen chopped basil
2 heaped tablespoons frozen chopped parsley
2 teaspoons frozen chopped ginger
2 tablespoons any vinegar
salt and freshly ground black pepper

I. Mix up the rub ingredients, and then pile onto the flesh side of the salmon fillets (not the skin side).

2. Heat the oil in a large frying pan over a medium heat, and swirl around the pan. One at a time, carefully place the salmon, spiced-side down, into the hot oil. Ensure the salmon sits nicely on the spices, so you get a nice crust once cooked. Cook for 3–4 minutes until nicely coloured.

3. Turn the heat right down, cover the pan with foil and cook for a further 3–4 minutes.

4. Turn off the heat and leave the salmon to rest in the pan for 3–4 minutes.

5. Meanwhile, place all the mayo ingredients into a blender and blitz until you have a lovely green, thick mayonnaise. Or if you don't have a blender, then just mix together really well.

6. Serve the salmon, skin-side down, with a little of the mayo.

WILD SALMON BURGERS

SERVES
4

PREP **15** *minutes plus chilling*
COOKING **6–8** *minutes*

FOR THE BURGERS

400g frozen Atlantic salmon, defrosted and
patted dry with kitchen paper, then very
finely chopped and chilled

1 egg white

1 tablespoon mayonnaise

1 tablespoon freshly grated ginger

1 tablespoon dark soy sauce

1 teaspoon toasted sesame oil

4 tablespoons breadcrumbs

salt and freshly ground black pepper

4 sesame buns, toasted, to serve

FOR THE MAYONNAISE

6–8 tablespoons mayonnaise

2–3 teaspoons wasabi

4–6 tablespoons finely chopped chives
(about 1 small bunch)

I'm a big fan of frozen salmon, particularly
the wild fish as it freezes and defrosts really
well. However, you need to be a little careful
when cooking it, as it can sometimes dry
out, especially if it is wild salmon. Ensure
you dry it really well on kitchen paper before
chopping. I add mayo to all my burgers: it
helps to keep the moisture in the burger.

1. In a bowl, mix together all the burger
ingredients, except the breadcrumbs, and
season well with salt and pepper. Add a few
breadcrumbs and mix really well, then chill for
20 minutes to firm up.

2. Preheat a grill to medium, or heat a frying
pan over a medium heat.

3. Mould the salmon mixture into four even
patties and grill or fry for 4–5 minutes on
each side.

4. Meanwhile, in a bowl, mix all the ingredients
for the mayo together really well.

5. Serve the burgers in toasted sesame buns
with a little of the wasabi mayo.

FRIED COCONUT PRAWNS
WITH MANGO & FETA SALSA

SERVES
4

PREP *20 minutes*
COOKING **5–10** *minutes*

FOR THE PRAWNS

4 tablespoons flour

2 eggs, beaten

150g panko breadcrumbs

150g desiccated coconut

16–18 large frozen shelled wild Atlantic prawns,
  defrosted (approx. 250g)

vegetable oil, for deep-frying

FOR THE SALSA

300g frozen mango, defrosted and
  finely chopped

1 small red onion, finely chopped

½ small red chilli, finely chopped

6 tablespoons frozen (or fresh) chopped
  coriander

finely grated zest and juice of 2 limes

150g feta cheese, crumbled

FOR THE MAYO

4 tablespoons mayonnaise

4 tablespoons tomato ketchup

1 tablespoon Sriracha sauce

2 teaspoons Cajun spice powder

I first cooked a version of this dish a couple of years ago for *This Morning* whilst in the Turks & Caicos islands, on a beach that had just been named the best in the world. Chef Colin Watson at the Sandals resort there used this flavour combination, so all credit goes to him. I sometimes serve it on a large slice of fresh watermelon in place of a plate. These prawns are amazing in every way and another fine example of how certain ingredients freeze really well!

1. Place the flour and eggs in separate bowls, then mix together the breadcrumbs and coconut in a different bowl. Coat the prawns in the flour, dip in the beaten egg and then dip in the breadcrumb mix.

2. In a bowl, mix all the ingredients for the salsa together well and leave to marinate.

3. In a small bowl, mix together all the ingredients for the mayo with a touch of water.

4. Heat a small pan of vegetable oil to 175°C. In batches, deep-fry the prawns for about 2–3 minutes until golden, then drain well on kitchen paper.

5. Serve hot with the salsa and mayo.

SPICY PRAWN & BASIL TAGLIERINI

SERVES
2

PREP *20 minutes*
COOKING *25 minutes*

2 tablespoons olive oil

1 large onion, finely chopped

2 garlic cloves, finely chopped

¼ teaspoon dried chilli flakes

400g can chopped tomatoes in juice

1 small jar peppers, drained (170g drained weight)

10g vegetable stock cube, crumbled

150g frozen shelled wild Atlantic prawns, roughly chopped

170g dried taglierini, cooked, kept warm and oiled (see page 58, step 2)

2 tablespoons frozen chopped basil

salt and freshly ground black pepper

Frozen wild prawns – either with the shell on or peeled – are superb. They keep their shape and flavour when defrosted and are really succulent. I often deep-fry them just coated in cornflour and they are delicious. They work well in lots of other dishes too, though this is a particularly easy one to prepare and cook.

I. Heat the oil in a frying pan over a medium heat. Add the onion, garlic, chilli flakes and chopped tomatoes, then cook for 3–4 minutes.

2. Meanwhile, place the peppers and stock cube in a blender and blitz until smooth.

3. Add to the onions, garlic and chilli. Bring to a simmer and cook for 5–6 minutes until slightly thickened.

4. Add the prawns and cook for 10 minutes.

5. Add the pasta and basil and stir though. Check the seasoning, then serve.

QUICK PRAWN, CORN & BEAN SAUTE

SERVES
2

PREP **10** *minutes*
COOKING **10-15** *minutes*

1 egg white
2 tablespoons cornflour
400g frozen shelled wild Atlantic prawns,
    defrosted and patted dry with kitchen paper
4-6 tablespoons any oil
200g frozen chopped onions
100g frozen sweetcorn
100g frozen broad beans
2 tablespoons poke sauce
2 teaspoons soy sauce
2 teaspoons fresh lime juice
4 tablespoons frozen chopped basil
freshly ground black pepper

When I tasted these wild prawns, they really blew me away. Their texture and flavour were amazing and if anybody thinks that frozen fish is second rate, then they need to buy and cook these little beauties. If I had a restaurant now, I'd buy the whole lot! This is not only a really filling dish but also a very colourful one. Just make sure you dry the prawns really well on kitchen paper before cooking them.

I. Mix the egg white and cornflour together well in a bowl and then add the prawns.

2. In a deep wok, heat the oil over a medium heat. Place the prawns, one by one, into the hot oil and sear well for 2–3 minutes, then turn over and seal on the other side for 2–3 minutes. Transfer to a plate.

3. Add the onions (you may need to add a little more oil) and cook over a high heat for a few minutes to get some quick colour, then add the sweetcorn and beans. Mix well.

4. Return the prawns to the pan along with the sauces, lime juice, basil and pepper. Sauté for a few minutes and check the seasoning. Serve straight away.

SARDINE RAREBIT

SERVES
4

PREP **10** *minutes*
COOKING **5–10** *minutes*

Quick, easy and straight to the point. Proving that a little canned fish can not only go a long way but also be incredibly tasty and easy to prepare and cook. Try this recipe with canned tuna, mackerel or even jackfruit.

2 × 120g can sardines in oil, drained
4 tablespoons mayonnaise
3 egg yolks
300g Cheddar, grated
4 thick slices of bread
pinch of smoked paprika
freshly ground black pepper

1. Preheat a grill to medium heat.

2. In a bowl, break up the sardines, but not too much, with a fork. Add the mayo, egg yolks and Cheddar and carefully mix together, trying not to break up the fish too much.

3. Toast the bread for a couple of minutes under the grill on one side only.

4. Pile on the fish mixture, making a nice dome in the middle.

5. Pop back under the grill and gently cook for 3–4 minutes until you have a nice glaze: take your time so it does not burn.

6. Slice and dust with smoked paprika.

CRAB, PEANUT & NOODLE SALAD

SERVES
4

PREP **25 minutes**
COOKING **none**

make ahead

FOR THE SALAD

100g (2 nests) dried instant rice noodles
400g frozen edamame beans, defrosted
2 × 150g cans crabmeat
4 tablespoons frozen chopped coriander
½ small cucumber, chopped into 5mm cubes

FOR THE DRESSING

2 tablespoons caster sugar
1 teaspoon fish sauce
2 tablespoons frozen chopped ginger
1 tablespoon brown miso paste
2 tablespoons soy sauce
pinch of dried chilli flakes

TO SERVE

2 large, ripe tomatoes, chopped
100g dry-roasted peanuts, chopped
lime wedges

A nice, tasty dish that has lots of texture and colour. In fact, it's even better if you leave it in the fridge overnight. I'm a big fan of canned crab; it can be a bit pricey but a little does go a long way.

1. Place the rice noodles in a bowl, cover with boiling water and leave to soften for 10 minutes.

2. Meanwhile, place the beans into a bowl with the crabmeat, coriander and cucumber and mix well.

3. Mix all the dressing ingredients together in a small bowl.

4. Drain the noodles well and run a knife through them to make shorter strands, then add to the beans. Pour the dressing over the noodles and mix well.

5. Serve in small bowls, topped with chopped tomatoes and peanuts and with lime wedges on the side.

CRAB & SWEETCORN WITH MELBA TOAST

SERVES
4

PREP **15** *minutes*
COOKING **30** *minutes*

I really like the taste and flavour of canned crab especially when it's paired with sweetcorn in any shape or form. Frozen chopped onions are handy when adding to a sauce when no browning is needed.

600ml milk
1 tablespoon vegetable oil
200g frozen chopped onions
1 small garlic clove, finely crushed
1 tablespoon frozen chopped coriander
pinch of chilli powder
55g unsalted butter, softened
50g plain flour
2 × 165g cans crabmeat, well drained
198g can sweetcorn, well drained
   (165g drained weight)
1 teaspoon anchovy essence (optional)
8 slices of white bread
200g panko or other breadcrumbs
100g Parmesan cheese, finely grated
salt and freshly ground black pepper

1. Pour the milk into a pan, then bring just to a boil.

2. Meanwhile, heat the oil in a frying pan over a low heat. Add the onion and garlic and cook for 2–3 minutes until softened but not browned. Then stir in the coriander and chilli powder.

3. In a bowl, mix together the butter and flour, then whisk into the hot milk really well. Take the pan off the heat.

4. Add the crabmeat to the white sauce with the sweetcorn, onion mixture and anchovy essence, if using, then season. Spoon the mixture into individual baking dishes and leave to cool.

5. Preheat the grill to medium.

6. Toast the bread under the grill for a few minutes on each side until golden brown. Cut off the crusts, then using a bread knife, cut through the middle of each slice of toast to split it into two extra-thin pieces.

7. Leave to slightly cool, then rub together the uncooked insides of the toast to remove any doughy or soggy crumbs. Halve diagonally.

8. Reduce the heat of the grill, then toast the uncooked sides of the bread for a few minutes until golden, crispy and crunchy.

9. Preheat the oven to 200°C/gas mark 6.

10. Sprinkle the breadcrumbs and grated cheese over the crab mixture in the dishes and cook in the oven for about 15 minutes or until heated through and the cheese has melted and nicely browned.

STORECUPBOARD STANDBYS

EGG-FREE (VEGAN) MAYONNAISE

MAKES
500ML

PREP **10 minutes**
COOKING **none**

make ahead

vegan

4 heaped teaspoons tarragon Dijon mustard
110ml soya milk
225ml olive oil or 50/50 olive oil and
    sunflower or rapeseed oil
50–75ml white wine vinegar
salt and freshly ground black pepper

This is probably one of the quickest recipes
I have ever made. Once all the ingredients
are in the jug, it takes just fifteen seconds
or so for everything to emulsify together
really well. I use different flavoured mustards
to change things a little; my current favourite
is tarragon.

1. Place all the ingredients into a measuring
jug. Blitz with a handheld blender: the whole
thing will come together nicely in seconds

2. Finally add enough water (about 100ml) to
form a nice consistency.

PINEAPPLE RELISH

SERVES
4

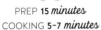
PREP **15** *minutes*
COOKING **5–7** *minutes*

make ahead

vegan

oil, for greasing
435g can pineapple, well drained
1 garlic clove, finely crushed
¼ teaspoon dried chilli flakes
juice of 1 lime
4 spring onions, finely chopped
1 red pepper, finely cubed
4 tablespoons extra virgin olive oil
2 tablespoons fresh mint
salt and freshly ground black pepper

Pineapple can be used in many ways, in both sweet and savoury dishes; canned is great for either. I serve this side with grilled or barbecued turkey or grilled fish. I also remove the onions and garlic and serve it with vanilla ice cream!

1. Heat a barbecue or large non-stick frying pan over a medium heat. Lightly oil the bars of the grill using a piece of kitchen paper dipped in a little oil.

2. Dry the pineapple really well with kitchen paper and then oil the pineapple.

3. Place the rings onto the grill or frying pan and gently cook for 2–3 minutes, then carefully turn over and cook for a further 3–4 minutes.

4. Place all the rest of the ingredients in a bowl and mix together well. Spoon over the grilled pineapple slices.

PUMPKIN, SWISS CHEESE & CUMIN SOUP

SERVES
4

PREP **15** *minutes*
COOKING **30** *minutes*

make ahead

vegetarian

An unusual but very tasty soup that is quick, easy and a little bit different. The secret is to toast the cumin seeds first to release all their wonderful aroma and to add the cheese at the *very last moment,* so it stays nice and stringy.

65g butter
250g frozen chopped onions
3 garlic cloves, 2 crushed, 1 halved
560g can potatoes, drained (345g drained weight)
2 × 425g cans pumpkin purée
1 teaspoon cumin seeds
2 × 10g vegetable stock cubes, crumbled
2 tablespoons vegetable oil
2 thick slices of bread, crusts removed and then cubed
milk (optional)
100g Gruyère cheese, finely grated
salt and freshly ground black pepper

I. Melt 50g of the butter in a large saucepan over a medium heat. Add the onions and crushed garlic, then cook for 2–3 minutes to soften, but do not allow to brown. Add the potatoes and pumpkin and mix well.

2. Heat a small frying pan over a low heat. Add the cumin seeds and cook for 3–4 minutes until they release their wonderful aroma: be careful they do not burn.

3. Add to the onion and potato mix, pour in enough water to cover the vegetables by 1cm (about 1 litre) and add the stock cubes. Bring to the boil, season then reduce to a simmer and cook for 10 minutes.

4. Meanwhile, heat the oil and the rest of the butter in a frying pan over a medium heat, then add the bread cubes and remaining halved garlic clove. Cook for 2–3 minutes until nicely browned, then tip into a colander and remove the garlic. Sprinkle with a little salt and pepper and keep warm.

5. Tip the soup into a blender and blitz until smooth, adding a little milk if it is too thick. Just before serving, stir in the cheese. Serve piping hot, scattered with the croutons.

SPICY BLACK-EYED PEAS & CORN

SERVES
4

PREP **25 minutes**
COOKING *none*

make ahead

400g can black-eyed peas, really well drained
340g can sweetcorn, well drained (285g drained weight)
4 spring onions, finely sliced
¼ teaspoon dried chilli flakes
½ teaspoon ground cumin
1 teaspoon garlic powder
½ teaspoon dried oregano
1 teaspoon onion powder
1–2 pinches of cayenne pepper (optional)
4 tablespoons frozen chopped coriander
2 tablespoons olive oil
2 tablespoons mayonnaise
salt and freshly ground black pepper

TO SERVE
tortilla chips
grilled or roasted chicken thighs

Canned beans are super versatile, handy, quick and really good for you. I had a version of this dish a few years ago in Texas, when they were served with fried chicken, but I also like to eat them as a snack with tortilla chips. No cooking is needed and if you can leave them for a few hours to marinate, then all the better. I tend to always have these dried herbs in my cupboard.

I. Place the drained beans, corn and spring onions into a bowl and mix well.

2. Add the rest of the ingredients and mix really well. Leave to marinate at room temperature for 20 minutes.

3. Stir well, season again and eat with tortilla chips and/or grilled chicken.

SIMPLE PLAIN WHITE LOAF

MAKES
1 LOAF

PREP **15** *minutes plus rising*
COOKING **15–20** *minutes*

make ahead

vegan

Simple and straight to the point and a real winner whenever I cook it on TV. It just shows that you need only four storecupboard ingredients plus water to make a really delicious loaf.

600g strong white flour,
     plus extra for dusting
1 teaspoon salt
2 tablespoons any oil
7g sachet dried yeast
300ml warm water

1. Place the flour, salt and oil into the bowl of a stand mixer and bring together.

2. Add the yeast and enough of the water to form a soft dough, mix well until the dough comes away from the sides of the bowl and the gluten forms a stretchy dough.

3. Tip onto a floured surface and knead well for 5 minutes.

4. Return the dough to the bowl, cover with clingfilm and leave until doubled in size (about 45 minutes).

5. Meanwhile preheat the oven to 220°C/gas mark 7.

6. Tip the dough onto the floured surface. This time just gently knead for a few seconds, just to bring together. Don't be rough.

7. Form into a sausage shape roughly the length of a 2lb loaf tin, then fold the edges under. Pop into the tin and press into the sides and base. Cover with clingfilm and leave to rise until almost doubled in size.

8. Dust with a little flour, then cut three diagonal slashes across the loaf and pop into the oven. Bake for about 15–20 minutes, or until well risen and browned.

9. Remove from the tin and leave to cool completely before slicing.

CHEESY BEANS ON EGGY BREAD

SERVES
2

PREP **15** *minutes*
COOKING **10** *minutes*

vegetarian

Beans on toast is one of my all-time favourites and still a go-to quick meal to this day. There is something really satisfying about making a meal using a can of baked beans and these recipes are easy and quick to make.

2 eggs
dash of milk
2–3 tablespoons any oil
2 slices of bread
2 teaspoons marmite
400g can baked beans, warmed
100g strong Cheddar, grated
salt and freshly ground black pepper

I. In a large bowl, beat the eggs and milk with salt and pepper.

2. Heat the oil in a large frying pan over a medium heat.

3. Dip both sides of the bread in the egg and then place into the hot oil. Fry for 3–4 minutes, then flip over and fry on the other side for 3–4 minutes.

4. Transfer to plates and evenly spread over a little marmite. Spoon over the warm beans and top with a little cheese.

MORE BEAN RECIPES →

Paprika chorizo beans PAGE 130

Coriander, chilli & honey baked beans on toast PAGE 130

Balti beans with mint & yoghurt PAGE 131

Cheesy beans on eggy bread PAGE 127

BBQ chicken, bean
& avocado quesadilla PAGE 130

CORIANDER, CHILLI & HONEY BAKED BEANS ON TOAST

 SERVES
2

 PREP **5** *minutes*
COOKING **5** *minutes*

 vegetarian

2 thick slices of bread or English muffins, halved and toasted
2 tablespoons soft salted butter
1 garlic clove (optional)
400g can baked beans
1 tablespoon softened unsalted butter
¼ teaspoon dried chilli flakes
1 tablespoon runny honey
4 tablespoons chopped fresh or frozen coriander (about 1 small bunch), plus extra to serve

I. Lightly toast the bread or muffins, then spread with the salted butter and rub with a little garlic, if using.

2. In a pan over a medium heat, warm the beans, with the unsalted butter, chilli flakes and honey for 2–3 minutes. Add the coriander, but do not warm through too much.

3. Top the toast with the beans and serve with more coriander.

PAPRIKA CHORIZO BEANS

 SERVES
2

 PREP **15** *minutes*
COOKING **12–15** *minutes*

1 tablespoon any oil
60g bellota chorizo pieces (use soft cooking chorizo if you can't find bellota chorizo)
1 small onion, finely chopped
2 thick slices of bread or English muffins, halved
2 tablespoons softened salted butter
400g can baked beans
2–3 tablespoons chopped fresh parsley

I. Heat a small pan over a low heat and add the oil, chorizo and onion. Cook for 10 minutes until the oils and paprika are released.

2. Meanwhile, toast the bread or muffins and spread with the butter.

3. Add the beans and warm through for 2–3 minutes, then finally add the parsley. Serve on the buttered toast or muffins.

BALTI BEANS WITH MINT & YOGURT

SERVES
2

PREP **10** *minutes*
COOKING **15** *minutes*

vegetarian

1 tablespoon Balti or other curry paste
400g can baked beans
1 tablespoon salted butter
1 tablespoon freshly chopped mint, plus
    extra to serve
1 naan, warmed
2–3 tablespoons yogurt
1 tablespoon mango chutney

1. Place the paste and beans into a pan over a medium heat and warm through for 2–3 minutes.

2. Add the butter, melt, then add the fresh mint.

3. Slice the warm naan nice and thin and place in bowls. Spoon over the beans, then top with a little yogurt, mango and more fresh mint.

BBQ CHICKEN, BEAN & AVOCADO QUESADILLA

SERVES
2

PREP **10** *minutes*
COOKING **10–15** *minutes*

400g can baked beans
pinch of dried chilli flakes
150g barbecue chicken, chopped into
    small pieces
1 small avocado, peeled, destoned and
    cut into small pieces
2 wheat tortillas

1. Place the beans and the chilli flakes in a small saucepan. Bring to a simmer and cook for 2–3 minutes until you have a thick mix.

2. Remove from the heat and stir in the chicken and avocado.

3. Place one tortilla into a quesadilla press, spread out the bean mix, then top with the second tortilla. Close the lid and cook for 6–8 minutes. Alternatively, use a frying pan lined with greaseproof paper (see page 24). Cook on each side for 3–4 minutes.

4. Open, cut into wedges and serve.

JACKET SPUD PRAWN COCKTAIL

SERVES
4

PREP **10** *minutes plus marinating*
COOKING **45** *minutes–1 hour*

Does what it says on the can although rather than baking the potatoes whole, I halve them to get a nice golden cut edge. I use as many frozen and storecupboard ingredients as possible here, and it works a treat.

FOR THE FILLING
200g mayonnaise
4 spring onions, finely chopped
2–3 tablespoons freshly chopped chives, plus
    extra to serve
2 teaspoons frozen chopped ginger
2 tablespoons frozen chopped coriander
2 tablespoons tomato ketchup
dash of Worcestershire sauce
dash of tabasco
250g frozen cooked prawns, defrosted
juice of ½ lemon
salt and freshly ground black pepper

FOR THE POTATOES
2 tablespoons any oil
4 large baking potatoes, halved widthways
50g melted butter
1 small firm lettuce such as Little Gem, Romaine
    or Cos, roughly chopped

1. Mix together the mayonnaise, spring onions, chives, ginger, coriander, tomato ketchup, Worcestershire sauce and tabasco in a large bowl.

2. Add the prawns and mix together, then season with salt and pepper and a little lemon juice to taste. If possible, leave to marinate in the fridge for 2–3 hours.

3. Preheat the oven to 220°C/gas mark 7.

4. Heat a large, ovenproof, non-stick frying pan over a medium heat and add the oil. Place the potatoes in the pan cut-side down and fry for a few minutes to get some colour.

5. Pop the pan into the oven, then bake for 45 minutes–1 hour, or until the potatoes are cooked through. Remove and set aside until cool enough to handle.

6. Carefully scoop out the cooked potato into a bowl, trying not to break the skins. Mix with the butter, lettuce and a little salt and pepper. Pile back into the potato skins, then spoon over the prawns and sprinkle with some more chives, if you want.

CHRISTMAS BURGER

SERVES
4

PREP **30** *minutes plus chilling*
COOKING **15-20** *minutes*

This was a bit of fun to make a few years ago on *This Morning* and it went down a storm. It uses pretty much everything from the freezer or the cupboard.

500g turkey thigh mince

2 tablespoons mayonnaise

2 tablespoons flour

4 eggs, 3 beaten

200g sage and onion stuffing mix

400g sausage meat

100g vacuum-packed or canned chestnuts, chopped

300g frozen mashed potatoes, defrosted

5–6 frozen cooked roasted potatoes, roughly chopped

16 frozen Brussels sprouts, defrosted and chopped

8 rashers crisp streaky bacon, spread with a dash of honey

salt and freshly ground black pepper

TO SERVE

4 sesame burger buns

finely shredded lettuce

4 tablespoons cranberry sauce

300ml thick poultry gravy, warmed

1. Mix the turkey mince really well with the mayo and some salt and pepper. Line a burger press with greaseproof paper, then press the mince into four even-sized burgers. Leave in the paper and chill in the fridge for 15 minutes.

2. Remove the paper, then dust in flour, dip into the beaten egg and coat well with the sage and onion stuffing mix. Return to the fridge.

3. In a bowl, mix the sausage meat really well with the chestnuts. Line the burger press with greaseproof paper, then press. Chill in the fridge with the burgers.

4. In a bowl, mix all the potatoes with the remaining egg and the Brussels sprouts. Shape into patties, then season well and chill in the fridge for 15 minutes.

5. In a frying pan over a medium heat, working in batches, cook the turkey burgers, sausage patties and potato patties for 5–6 minutes, turning carefully. Keep warm in the oven, then fry the bacon in the pan for a few minutes.

6. Layer the patties and bacon in the buns, top with the lettuce and cranberry sauce. Stick a skewer in the centre to hold it all together and cut in half. Serve with the gravy for dipping.

CAN CAN BEAN CHILLI

SERVES
4

PREP **15 minutes**
COOKING **20–25 minutes**

make ahead

vegan

2 tablespoons olive oil
1 onion, finely chopped
1 garlic clove, crushed
1 teaspoon ground cumin
¼ teaspoon dried chilli flakes
½ teaspoon paprika
½ teaspoon ground cinnamon
400g can chopped tomatoes in juice
400g can kidney beans, drained and rinsed
400g can black beans, drained and rinsed
400g can haricot beans, drained and rinsed
10g vegetable stock cube, crumbled
salt and freshly ground black pepper
2 × 250g packets microwaveable
    long-grain rice, warmed, to serve

Every cook needs to have a chilli recipe of some description and, to be frank, I never tire of cooking or eating chilli. Yes, I eat a lot of microwaveable rice sachets and they are brilliant in every way: done in two minutes.

1. Heat the oil in a large, heavy-based pan over a medium heat. Sauté the onion, garlic and spices for 3–4 minutes until soft.

2. Add the tomatoes, 100ml water, all the beans and the stock cube and really mix well. Bring to the boil and then gently simmer for 15–20 minutes.

3. Season well with salt and pepper and serve with the warmed rice.

BACON, ONION & POTATO QUICHE

SERVES
6-8

PREP **10 minutes**
COOKING **45-50 minutes**

make ahead

2 tablespoons any oil

4 rashers back bacon, cut into very small pieces

2 onions, finely chopped

568ml milk

500g frozen shortcrust pastry, defrosted,
   lined in a 24cm × 4cm-deep flan tin, then
   blind baked and sealed with egg wash
   (see page 82, steps 1–4)

560g can potatoes, drained (345g drained
   weight) and cut into small cubes

2 tablespoons frozen chopped parsley

250g Gruyère or Emmental cheese,
   finely grated

4 eggs

pinch of ground nutmeg

salt and freshly ground black pepper

Another example of how canned potatoes can make a really nice filling for a quiche. You may think washing, peeling, boiling and draining the spud is all fine, but it's much easier to just open a can – and you get a pretty good end result!

1. Preheat the oven to 180°C/gas mark 4.

2. Heat the oil and in a frying pan over a medium heat. Fry the bacon for 10 minutes, add the onions, then cook for a further 5 minutes.

3. Meanwhile, pour the milk into a pan and bring to the boil, then leave to cool for 10 minutes.

4. Spread the bacon mix over the base of the pastry. Sprinkle over the cubed potatoes, then the parsley, then top with the cheese.

5. In a bowl, gently whisk the eggs with the hot milk and nutmeg and season with salt and pepper. Pour half over the cheese.

6. Place the pastry on a baking tray, place in the oven and then fill the case with the remaining egg and milk mix. This way, you avoid any spillage.

7. Bake for 25–30 minutes, but do not soufflé.

TOMATO SOUP,
HAM & CHEESE QUICHE

SERVES
6–8

PREP **20** *minutes*
COOKING **35–40** *minutes*

make ahead

Using canned soup sounds a bit strange but trust me, it does work. It gives the quiche a lovely, deep sweet tomato flavour. It takes a little longer to set than many quiches (as you have to cook it slightly slower), but the texture once cooked is far softer and lighter.

500g frozen shortcrust pastry, defrosted, lined in a 24cm × 4cm-deep flan tin, then blind baked (see page 82, steps 1–3)
1 egg, beaten
2 tablespoons any oil
3 onions, very finely chopped
300g wafer thin cooked ham, cut into small pieces
275g Cheddar cheese, coarsely grated
2 medium eggs
2 medium egg yolks
300ml milk, boiled and cooled for 10 minutes
400g can tomato soup, warmed
1–2 pinches of ground nutmeg
salt and freshly ground black pepper

1. Preheat the oven to 180°C/gas mark 4.

2. Brush the pastry case with the beaten egg and place in the oven for 10 minutes.

3. Meanwhile, heat the oil in a pan over a medium heat. Add the onions and cook for 10 minutes.

4. Spread the onions over the base of the pastry case, then top with the ham and cheese.

5. In a bowl, beat together the eggs and egg yolks, then add the milk and tomato soup. Season with salt, pepper and nutmeg.

6. Pour half over the cheese, ham and onions.

7. Place the quiche on a baking tray, then place in the oven. Now pour in the remaining egg mix – this way you avoid spillage.

8. Bake for 25–30 minutes. Leave to slightly cool before cutting.

FREE-FORM POTATO, RED ONION, MAYO & PESTO TART

SERVES
4

PREP **30** *minutes*
COOKING **45–50** *minutes*

VEGETARIAN
if using veggie pesto

A nice and easy, quick lunchtime or dinner dish. This can be cooked ahead and left to eat at room temperature along with, say, a tomato and onion or simple green salad. An easy lunchtime or dinner dish.

2–3 tablespoons any oil
2 red onions, very thinly sliced
500g sheet ready-rolled puff pastry
plain flour, for dusting
4 tablespoons red pesto
400g cooked potato, thinly sliced (skin on is fine)
salt and freshly ground black pepper

FOR THE MAYONNAISE
(ensure all the below are at room temperature)
2 egg yolks
2 tablespoons white wine vinegar
1 tablespoon Dijon mustard
200ml any oil
salt and freshly ground black pepper

1. Preheat the oven to 200°C/gas mark 6.

2. Heat the oil in a frying pan over a medium heat and gently sauté the onions for 10 minutes until slightly softened.

3. Roll out the pastry on a floured worksurface until it is roughly 35cm × 25cm; don't worry too much about the shape. Dock well, then place onto a non-stick baking tray.

4. Place the egg yolks in a liquidiser and add the vinegar, mustard, 1 tablespoon of water and a little salt and pepper. Blitz for 20 seconds, then gradually add the oil in a thin stream while blitzing until the mix thickens. Spoon into a bowl and set aside.

5. Spoon a thin, even layer of mayo onto the pastry, then add a little of the pesto. Lay over the cooked potato slices and then the onions. Dot over a little more pesto and season with salt and pepper.

6. Bake in the oven for 35–40 minutes until the pastry is nicely browned and cooked. Remove and leave to slightly cool before cutting. Serve with the rest of the mayo and pesto.

SOMETHING SWEET

BLACKCURRANT JAM ROLL

SERVES
6

PREP **20** *minutes*
COOKING **45** *minutes*

make ahead

Steamed suet roll is one of the greatest, if not *the* greatest, winter puddings. When prepared and cooked correctly, it is an absolute joy to eat. But when it's not, it's the worst pudding in the world. To avoid disaster, there are two important things to note. One: ensure you use plenty of jam; the more the better. Believe me, there is nothing worse than a mean jam roll. Two: serve not with trendy anglaise but Bird's – yes Bird's – custard; it's the best custard by far. A final tip: sweeten the custard with golden syrup rather than sugar for a lovely twist.

butter, for greasing
225g self-raising flour
pinch of salt
115g suet
55g caster sugar
1 egg, lightly beaten
100g blackcurrant jam
200g frozen blackcurrants
hot custard, to serve

**IF YOU HAVE ANY
JAM ROLL LEFT OVER**
▶ Wrap in clingfilm and chill. When needed, slice cold and warm in a microwave on medium power, taking care, as the jam can burn.

1. Prepare a 24cm steamer filled with boiling water. This is very important: the pastry must be cooked as soon as it is ready, or you will end up with a heavy, leaden end product. Tear off two roughly 30 × 40cm pieces of foil and butter really well.

2. Place the flour, salt, suet, sugar and egg in a mixing bowl and mix well. Add a touch of cold water and mix to a soft but not sticky dough.

3. Straight away, roll out the pastry until it measures about 30 × 40cm. Evenly spread over the jam, then sprinkle over the frozen blackcurrants. Roll up nice and lightly, not too tight, then halve widthways.

4. Place on top of the prepared foil. Roll loosely around each roll (to allow it to expand), then twist up the ends.

5. Place in the steamer and steam for about 40 minutes until the rolls are tight and firm (gently squeeze to test). If they are not done, just leave for a few more minutes. Carefully remove from the steamer, and leave to set.

6. Open the foil and slice each roll into three. Serve with hot custard sweetened with a little golden syrup.

WHITE CHOCOLATE MUFFINS

MAKES
8

PREP **15** *minutes*
COOKING **15-20** *minutes*

make ahead

vegetarian

Tomato soup? Yes, it does work, bizarre as it sounds! Just mix together the wet and dry ingredients and bake. However, take care not to overmix or the muffins will be tough and chewy.

DRY INGREDIENTS
2 teaspoons baking powder
2 teaspoons bicarbonate of soda
300g plain flour
80g sugar
200g white chocolate, chopped

WET INGREDIENTS
3 eggs
1 teaspoon vanilla extract
100ml skimmed milk
400g can tomato soup

1. Preheat the oven to 180°C/gas mark 4. Line an eight-hole muffin tin with cases.

2. Mix together the baking powder, bicarb, flour, sugar and chocolate until well combined.

3. In a separate bowl, mix together the eggs, vanilla, milk and tomato soup until well combined.

4. Add the egg mixture to the bowl of flour and lightly mix.

5. Spoon into the lined muffin tin, then bake for 15–20 minutes until well risen and soft to the touch. Do not overcook or the muffins will be dry.

6. Remove from the oven and leave to cool.

ICED CINNAMON BUNS

MAKES
9 buns

PREP **15-20** *minutes plus proving*
COOKING **25-40** *minutes*

MAKE AHEAD
freezable

vegetarian

These tear-and-share buns taste and look quite spectacular, but are simple to make; just remember to take your time and don't rush. Once cooked these freeze really well.

250g strong bread flour
350g plain flour, plus extra for dusting
1–2 pinches of salt
80g caster sugar
10g dried yeast
6 teaspoons ground cinnamon
80g salted butter, melted, plus extra for
    greasing
225–300ml full-fat milk, warmed
150g dark brown sugar
6–8 tablespoons fondant icing sugar

1. Place the flours, salt, sugar, yeast and 2 teaspoons of the cinnamon into a bowl. Mix well, then add the melted butter and 225ml of the milk and mix to a soft dough. Add more milk if needed; if the dough is too dry (and tight) it will be difficult to roll it out.

2. Knead well in a floured bowl for 2–3 minutes, then cover with clingfilm and leave to prove for about 30–40 minutes until doubled in size.

3. Turn the dough out onto a floured surface and gently roll out, carefully stretching until you have a roughly 30cm square. Don't go mad here or the gluten will tighten and the dough will not roll or stretch out.

4. Mix the brown sugar and remaining cinnamon together and sprinkle over the dough right to the edges. Roll up the dough until you have a long sausage shape. Cut into nine pieces and place, spaced for the dough to expand, onto a lightly greased, round tray. Cover with clingfilm and leave to prove for about 30–40 minutes until doubled in size.

5. Preheat the oven to 220°C/gas mark 7.

6. Carefully remove the clingfilm and pop the tray into the oven. Bake for 10 minutes to give the buns an initial lift.

7. Turn down the heat to 200°C/gas mark 6 and bake for a further 15–20 minutes or until cooked through and well browned. Remove from the oven and leave to cool on a wire rack.

8. Mix the fondant sugar with enough water to make a thin icing: you want to see the lovely circles of the buns. Paint all over the finished buns and let it drizzle all down the sides: don't be shy. Leave to set, then tear and share.

SQUIDGY CREME EGG BROWNIE

SERVES
4-6

PREP **20 minutes plus chilling**
COOKING **40-45 minutes**

make ahead

vegetarian

2 tablespoons golden syrup

110g salted butter, softened

150g caster sugar

150g bitter chocolate

75g plain flour, sifted

4 eggs, at room temperature

finely grated zest of 1 large orange

4 Creme Eggs, halved

vanilla ice cream, to serve (optional)

All the ingredients except the fresh orange zest are from the storecupboard. Just remember to allow the brownie to cool a little after taking out of the oven – or, better yet, chill in the fridge – or it will be too soft to cut.

1. Preheat the oven to 180°C/gas mark 4. Line a 20cm square baking tray with greaseproof paper, or oil well.

2. Melt the golden syrup, butter, sugar and chocolate together in a bowl set over a pan of simmering water.

3. Remove the bowl from the pan, then stir in the flour, eggs and orange zest. Mix well but do not overmix or the finished brownie will be chewy.

4. Pour into the prepared tray, then carefully place the eight Creme Egg halves into the top of the mix, pressing down slightly.

5. Pop into the oven and cook for 35–40 minutes.

6. Remove from the oven and leave to cool, then chill in the fridge for 30 minutes before cutting. Serve with vanilla ice cream, if you like.

HONEYCOMB ICE CREAM

SERVES
6

PREP **15** *minutes + chilling & freezing*
COOKING **5** *minutes*

make ahead

vegetarian

A delicious no-churn ice cream recipe that couldn't be easier. If you want a slightly firmer ice cream, just reduce the syrup or honey or take out altogether and add a little more cream.

1 tablespoon vanilla extract
350g can condensed milk
5 tablespoons golden syrup or runny honey
500ml double cream, lightly whipped
    (don't go mad: it needs to be soft)
200g dark chocolate
2 × 40g Crunchies, chopped into small pieces

1. Mix the vanilla extract with the condensed milk and golden syrup. Add the whipped cream and gently whisk together.

2. Pour into a large, freezer-proof container (ideally large enough to fit the ice cream 2–3cm deep, to freeze quicker). Freeze until soft.

3. Melt the chocolate in a bowl over a pan of simmering water. Remove from the heat, then add the small pieces of honeycomb to the chocolate. Mix with a fork to coat, then place onto a baking tray lined with greaseproof paper. Chill in the fridge until set.

4. Remove the ice cream and gently whisk or beat with a fork. Return to the freezer for a further 45–50 minutes. Beat again, then add the honeycomb and freeze until set.

MINT CHOC CHIP ICE CREAM

SERVES
6

 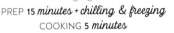
PREP **15 minutes + chilling & freezing**
COOKING **5 minutes**

make ahead

vegetarian

1 tablespoon peppermint extract, or more
   to taste
350g can condensed milk
5 tablespoons golden syrup or runny honey
500ml of double cream, lightly whipped
   (don't go mad: it needs to be soft)
150g bitter chocolate
8 After Eight chocolates, chopped
   into 5mm cubes

Another great way to make a super soft ice cream if you don't have a machine. Make it your own by swapping out the peppermint and chocolates for any other flavours you want.

1. In a bowl, mix the peppermint extract with the condensed milk and golden syrup. Add the whipped cream and gently whisk together.

2. Pour into a large, freezer-proof container (ideally large enough to fit the ice cream 2–3cm deep, to freeze quicker). Freeze until soft.

3. Melt the bitter chocolate in a bowl over a pan of simmering water, then set aside.

4. Remove the ice cream and add the small pieces of chopped After Eights, then drizzle over the melted chocolate. It should set pretty much straight away, so swirl it in and break it up.

5. Return to the freezer for a further 45–50 minutes. Whisk so you have a soft ice cream and serve.

Honeycomb ice cream PAGE 150

Mint choc chip ice cream PAGE 151

GYPSY TART

SERVES
6-8

PREP **10** *minutes*
COOKING **10** *minutes*

make ahead

vegetarian

When I was a child, gypsy tart was often on the lunch menu at my school in East Kent. I have to confess, I hated it at the time as I found it way too sickly. However, after filming for ITV's *This Morning* at The Sportsman, in Seasalter, Kent, with proprietor and great friend Stephen Harris, I changed my mind. We discussed said dish in great depth and his version was a revelation – light, airy and perfectly balanced. The two golden rules are: chill the evaporated milk overnight or it will not whip; and do not brush the inside of the cooked pastry case with egg (you would normally do this to stop it going soggy). If you do, the tart filling will shrink away from the pastry once cooked.

400g can evaporated milk, well chilled (ideally overnight in the fridge)
320g soft dark brown sugar
500g frozen shortcrust pastry, defrosted, lined in a 25cm × 4cm-deep flan tin, then blind baked (see page 82, steps 1–3)
20 pecan halves, lightly toasted
finely grated zest of 2 large lemons
200g full-fat crème fraîche

1. Preheat the oven to 160°C/gas mark 3.

2. Pour the evaporated milk and sugar in a bowl and beat with an electric whisk for about 10 minutes until really thick and glossy.

3. Spoon the mixture into the pastry case and decorate the top with the toasted pecan halves, spacing them evenly apart.

4. Bake in the oven for 10 minutes until risen and golden, then leave to cool to room temperature.

5. Meanwhile, stir the lemon zest into the crème fraîche.

6. Serve the tart in wedges with a spoonful of crème fraîche on top – adding a squeeze of lemon juice, if liked.

VIENNETTA

SERVES
4

PREP **20** *minutes*
COOKING **10** *minutes*

make ahead

vegetarian

My twist on this iconic dessert. If I'm honest, it takes a bit of time to get it right, but it's quite pleasing to prepare and make. You need to be careful to pipe as quickly as possible once the mix is ready, as the meringue will start to break down. Freeze overnight if you can. Of course, if you don't want to go to all that trouble, you could just buy one!

6 egg whites (185g), at room temperature
pinch of cream of tartar
175g caster sugar
300ml double cream, whipped
100ml bitter chocolate, melted then cooled

1. Wrap a baking tray in several layers of clingfilm. Cut a piece of paper 23cm × 10cm, place on the clingfilm so you have a template, then cover nice and tightly with clingfilm. Prepare a piping bag with a large, flat, plain nozzle.

2. Place the egg whites into a bowl with the cream of tartar and whisk until nice and foamy.

3. Add half the sugar and whisk to a really firm meringue. Rain in the last of the sugar and whisk again until really thick and glossy.

4. Carefully fold into the double cream until incorporated.

5. Spoon into the piping bag and pipe from side to side on the paper template.

6. Down the middle, spoon some of the melted chocolate. Pipe again and repeat with the chocolate.

7. Finally pipe and swirl down the centre of the Viennetta, flick over a little chocolate and freeze until really firm, ideally overnight.

8. Slice and serve.

FROZEN BLUEBERRY TART

SERVES
6-8

PREP **30 minutes plus chilling**
COOKING **35-40 minutes**

make ahead

vegetarian

If you want this tart to have a deep colour and flavour, it's essential to use frozen blueberries – you don't get the same result from puréed fresh berries. Blackberries, raspberries and blackcurrants are also far nicer when defrosted from frozen, not only in colour but also flavour. When defrosting, the cells of the fruit break down and you get a superb, dark-coloured juice. So here is a light flan that looks stunning once cooked.

300ml single cream
600g frozen blueberries, defrosted
312g jar lemon curd
75g caster sugar
4 egg yolks
1 egg
½ teaspoon cornflour
500g frozen shortcrust pastry, defrosted,
    lined in a 24cm × 4cm-deep flan tin, then
    blind baked and sealed with egg wash
    (see page 82, steps 1–4)
finely grated zest of 1 large lemon

1. Preheat the oven to 160°C/gas mark 3.

2. In a pan, heat the cream until just boiling, then remove from the heat.

3. Place 350g of the defrosted blueberries, half the lemon curd and the caster sugar into a blender and blitz until smooth. Pour into a bowl.

4. Place the egg yolks, whole egg and cornflour in a bowl and just combine. Add the warm cream and bring just together.

5. Carefully pour into the cooked pastry case and bake in the oven for 25–35 minutes or until just set. Remove and chill well in the fridge for 2 hours, or best overnight.

6. When ready to serve, mix the rest of the blueberries with the rest of the jar of lemon curd and the lemon zest. Spoon over the tart, then cut and serve.

MANCHESTER TART

SERVES
4-6

PREP *25 minutes plus chilling*
COOKING *20 minutes*

make ahead

vegetarian

An old school favourite of mine along with Gypsy Tart (see page 154): really easy to make and tastes delicious. Ensure the custard is slightly thicker than you would normally make it, so the tart is easier to cut.

6 tablespoons seedless raspberry jam
350g frozen shortcrust pastry, defrosted, lined in a 36 × 12 × 2.5cm-deep loose-based baking tin, then blind baked and sealed with egg wash (see page 82, steps 1–4)
2 egg yolks
6 tablespoons caster sugar
4–5 tablespoons (60g) custard powder
1 teaspoon vanilla extract
300ml full-fat milk
400g can 55%-fat coconut milk
80g desiccated coconut, lightly toasted

1. Evenly spread the jam over the bottom of the cooked pastry case.

2. Place the egg yolks, sugar, custard powder and vanilla into a bowl and whisk together.

3. Place the milks into a saucepan and add a couple of tablespoons to the egg yolk mix. Place the saucepan over the heat and bring to a simmer. Whisk in the rest of the egg yolk mixture, then bring back to a simmer for 5–10 minutes until nice and thick.

4. Pour straight into the pastry case and spread out nice and evenly, then leave to cool. Chill in the fridge for 30 minutes.

5. Once chilled, evenly spread the desiccated coconut over the top and serve in slices.

UPSIDE DOWN PINEAPPLE & LAVENDER PUDDING CAKE

SERVES
6–8

PREP **10 minutes**
COOKING **25–30 minutes**

make ahead

vegetarian

A real classic. I remember my mother making this for Sunday lunch many years ago, although she did not use lavender in hers. I added the fresh lavender after cooking at Castle Farm in Kent for ITV's *This Morning*.

300g caster sugar
8 rings canned pineapple, drained really well
6–8 sprigs fresh lavender, flowers picked (optional)
3 eggs, at room temperature
125g self-raising flour
125g unsalted butter, melted
ice cream or crème fraîche, to serve (optional)

1. Preheat the oven to 180°C/gas mark 4. Line a 28 × 24cm non-stick baking tray.

2. Place 200g of the sugar into a medium-sized, non-stick frying pan, add a little water and then place over a medium heat until caramelised: the sugar will melt, then it will turn into a light caramel.

3. Carefully pour the caramel into the baking tray and spread evenly, then leave to cool.

4. Place the pineapple rings onto the cooled caramel, then fill the centres with the lavender, if using.

5. Place the eggs and the rest of the sugar together in a bowl and whisk until it becomes light ribbons. Add the flour and then the melted butter and gently mix.

6. Pour the batter over the pineapple and lavender. Bake for 25–30 minutes, or until light golden brown and well risen.

7. Remove from the oven, then leave to cool for 10 minutes before carefully turning out. Eat warm with ice cream or crème fraîche – or both!

PRUNE & BRANDY MERINGUE PIE

SERVES
6-8

PREP **15** *minutes*
COOKING **50-55** *minutes*

make ahead

vegetarian

Using a great combination of tinned prunes and brandy, this pie is a very tasty change from a normal lemon meringue pie. I first ate a version of this pie in the early 90s at a 2-Michelin-star restaurant in France. At the time it was really popular, but I hadn't had one in so long that I had forgotten how nice it was. My mum and dad still eat tinned prunes.

FOR THE BASE

420g can prunes in syrup, drained and stoned
2 tablespoons brandy
2 eggs
2 egg yolks
284ml whipping cream
50g caster sugar
squeeze of lemon juice
350g frozen shortcrust pastry, defrosted,
    lined in a 24.5cm × 2.5cm-deep flan tin,
    then blind baked and sealed with egg wash
    (see page 82, steps 1–4)

FOR THE MERINGUE

100g egg whites (from 3–4 eggs)
pinch of cream of tartar
50g caster sugar
50g icing sugar, sifted
granulated sugar, for sprinkling
thick pouring cream

I. Preheat the oven to 170°C/gas mark 3.

2. Place the prunes in a liquidiser with the brandy and whizz until you have a very thick purée. Spoon the purée into a bowl, add the whole eggs and yolks and mix well. Add the cream, sugar and lemon juice and whisk until smooth. Pour into the pastry case.

3. Place on a baking tray and bake in the oven for about 35 minutes or until just set. The pie should be slightly wobbly right in the centre; the residual heat will finish off the cooking. Do not overcook or the pie may souffle and split. Remove from the oven.

4. Turn up the oven 220°C/gas mark 7.

5. To make the meringue, whisk the egg whites and cream of tartar in the bowl of a stand mixer on a moderate speed until thick and creamy. Add the caster sugar, then continue to whisk until thick and glossy. Finally add the icing sugar and whisk well.

6. Pipe or evenly spoon onto the top of the pie, sprinkle over a little granulated sugar, then bake in the oven for about 2–3 minutes until the meringue is firm to the touch and lightly browned. Serve with thick pouring cream.

PEAR, CHERRY & CHOCOLATE FRYING PAN PUDDING

SERVES
4

PREP **10 minutes**
COOKING **12 minutes**

vegetarian

One of the first recipes I cooked on *Ready Steady Cook* many years ago. It's a great, easy one-pot pudding. I love canned fruit in any form including strawberries and raspberries. Canned cherries take me back to my first job in a seaside hotel where they were used to make a sauce to serve with roast duck.

400g can pears, drained and sliced
400g can cherries, drained
4 egg whites, at room temperature, separated
pinch of cream of tartar
150g caster sugar
4 egg yolks
1 tablespoon sifted cocoa powder, plus
    extra to serve
2 tablespoons sifted cornflour
100g dark chocolate, melted

TO SERVE
200ml single cream
icing sugar, for dusting

1. Preheat the oven to 220°C/gas mark 7. Lightly oil a 24cm ovenproof, non-stick frying pan.

2. Place the pears into the prepared pan, then sprinkle over the cherries. Set aside.

3. In the bowl of a stand mixer, whisk the egg whites with the cream of tartar for 3–4 minutes until foamy and thick. Add the sugar and whisk until thick and glossy.

4. Remove from the machine, then carefully fold in the egg yolks, cocoa and cornflour.

5. Evenly spoon the meringue over the pears and cherries, then place the pan into the oven and cook for 10–12 minutes, or until risen and just undercooked in the middle.

6. Remove from the oven and pour the melted chocolate all over. Serve with cream and dust with icing sugar and cocoa. Eat straight from the pan.

PIMM'S TRIFLE

SERVES
4-6

PREP *20 minutes plus chilling*
COOKING *10 minutes*

MAKE AHEAD
chill after step 4

vegetarian

I love Pimm's but had never cooked with it until I thought about using it in this summer trifle, and it works perfectly. I've used pretty much all the ingredients for the famous summer drink – apart from the cucumber. Thickening the instant custard with white chocolate is a real winner.

350ml Pimm's
2 × 75g packets instant custard
500g white chocolate, 350g finely chopped,
    150g grated
finely grated zest 2 oranges
12 trifle sponges
4 tablespoons strawberry jam
250g fresh ripe strawberries, sliced,
    plus 6 strawberries, halved
150g caster sugar
large bunch of fresh mint, roughly chopped
750ml double cream
4-6 tablespoons icing sugar
2 teaspoons vanilla extract

1. In a pan, warm 200ml of the Pimm's, then make up the custard according to the packet instructions but using 50/50 boiling water and Pimm's. Once thickened, whisk in the chopped chocolate and mix well until melted, then finally add the orange zest. Set aside.

2. Halve the sponges horizontally, spread evenly with the strawberry jam, then replace the tops. Cut into small cubes, put half in the bottom of a large bowl, then pour over the rest of the Pimm's.

3. Sprinkle over half the strawberries and cover with half the custard-chocolate mix. Add the rest of the sponge and whole strawberries and then top with the rest of the custard.

4. Chill well for 2 hours or best overnight.

5. Meanwhile, in a pan mix together the caster sugar and 200ml water. Boil for 3 minutes until thick, then leave to cool. Add the mint and then blitz with a handheld blender. Set aside.

6. When ready to serve, whip the double cream, icing sugar and vanilla together; do not over whip. Pile most of the cream onto the set trifle. Sprinkle with the grated chocolate, decorate with the halved strawberries and pipe rosettes of the remaining cream. At the last moment, spoon over the fresh mint syrup.

SAUTEED PEACHES
WITH LEMON & YOGURT

SERVES
4

PREP **5** *minutes*
COOKING **10-15** *minutes*

make ahead

vegetarian

Warming canned peaches in a little syrup and nutmeg is such a simple way of creating a delicious dessert. All you need is a little thick yogurt. Griddling the peaches first isn't essential but makes for a prettier look.

411g can peach halves in syrup
2 teaspoons vegetable oil
2 tablespoons light brown sugar
pinch of ground nutmeg
juice of 2 large lemons
200g thick natural sheep's yogurt

1. Drain the peaches, reserving 6 tablespoons of their syrup, then dry well using kitchen paper.

2. Heat a barbecue or large, non-stick griddle pan over a medium heat. Brush the bars with some kitchen paper dipped in a little vegetable oil, or add the oil to the pan. Grill the peaches, cut side down, for a few minutes.

3. Meanwhile heat the sugar and peach syrup in a large, non-stick frying pan over a medium heat for 2–3 minutes. Increase the heat to high and cook for about 4–5 minutes until the sugar starts to bubble.

4. Add the nutmeg, then place the grilled peaches in the pan, cut-side down, and reduce the heat to medium. Sauté for about 2 minutes, or until golden brown. Turn the peaches over and cook for a further 1–2 minutes.

5. Add the lemon juice and simmer for 2–3 minutes.

6. To serve, divide the peach halves between four bowls and top with spoonfuls of the yogurt.

WARM PEARS
WITH CONDENSED MILK & LIME

SERVES
4

PREP **10** *minutes*
COOKING **10** *minutes*

VEGETARIAN
if using veggie wine

This recipe is so simple yet delicious.
Any wine will do and the whole dish is nice
and light. A piece of shortbread is a great
accompaniment.

187ml bottle of rosé or white wine
finely grated zest and juice of 2 limes
400g can pears, drained well
450g condensed milk
25g toasted chopped hazelnuts

I. Place the wine and lime juice (not zest) in
a pan over a medium heat with the pears and
warm through for 3-4 minutes.

2. Add the condensed milk and warm through.
Serve in deep bowls and sprinkle over the lime
zest and chopped hazelnuts.

COFFEE CRÈME BRULÉE

SERVES
6

PREP **10** *minutes plus chilling*
COOKING **40** *minutes*

MAKE AHEAD

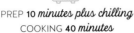

vegetarian

I love crème brulée, but when I choose it from a menu, nine times out of ten it's really disappointing – normally because the custard is too thick and stodgy. I use just egg yolks, and only 4–5 per 600ml of cream, to get a perfect consistency. Also I use whipping cream, as double is too thick and rich to get a good, soft end result.

600ml whipping cream
1 tablespoon instant coffee granules
5 egg yolks
170g can condensed milk
finely grated zest of 1 large lemon
caster sugar, for glazing

1. Preheat the oven to 150°C/gas mark 2.

2. Pour the whipping cream and coffee granules into a pan. Bring to a simmer, stirring occasionally, then remove from the heat.

3. Place the egg yolks and condensed milk into a bowl and bring together with a whisk; don't go mad. Gradually whisk in the coffee cream, then add the lemon zest.

4. Place six 7.5cm × 4cm-deep ramekins or cocotte dishes into a deep baking tray. Divide the mix equally between the ramekins.

5. Carefully pour boiling water into the tray halfway up the sides of the ramekins. Cover with foil and carefully transfer the tray to the oven. Cook for 25–30 minutes or until just cooked and wobbly.

6. Uncover, then carefully lift the ramekins out of the water bath. Leave to cool for 30 minutes, then chill in the fridge for 2 hours.

7. Just before serving, place a *very* thin layer of sugar over each custard and gently melt until browned using a blow torch. Leave to cool, then repeat with a second, thin layer of sugar. Leave to cool, then serve.

SPICED PUMPKIN LATTE

All the rage at the moment. Here's my version, including how to make the cappuccino froth using only a jam jar and a microwave...

425g can pumpkin purée
2–3 tablespoons coffee granules (I like my coffee to be strong, but it's up to personal taste)
3–4 tablespoons soft brown sugar or maple syrup, or a mix of both
2 teaspoons ground mixed spice
400ml semi-skimmed milk
1 teaspoon ground cinnamon
2 tablespoons mini fudge pieces
whipped cream (optional)

1. Spoon the pumpkin purée into a large, microwave-safe bowl and whisk to break it up, then pop into the microwave and warm through for 1–2 minutes – it doesn't need to be boiling hot. Keep warm.

2. Boil 600ml water, then pour over the coffee granules. Stir to dissolve, then add the sugar and mixed spice and mix well.

3. Here's the clever bit: pour half the milk into a jam jar and screw the lid on well. Vigorously shake the jar for 30–45 seconds until it foams up. Remove the lid and then heat the jar in the microwave for 15–20 seconds at 600 watts. Keep an eye on it – the foam will rise to the top of the jar. Remove the jar from the microwave and gently fold the foam and liquid together.

4. Pour the hot pumpkin and coffee mix into four tall glasses, leaving 2–3cm at the top. Spoon the jam jar milk evenly between two of the filled glasses, right to the top.

5. Repeat the microwave process with the remaining milk and spoon over the last two glasses.

6. Dust with cinnamon and add a few fudge pieces and some whipped cream, if you like.

INDEX

index

And THANK YOU

A book like this doesn't just happen; it involves a lot of hard work from a lot of people. So a big thank you to Kate Whitaker – as ever, great pics – along with Jules Mercer, for understanding exactly what I want to create: relaxed simple food for everybody to enjoy.

Helen Bratby, for a really cool design that will be timeless. Claire Rogers, thanks for not hassling me too much and understanding my sometimes peculiar way of writing recipes. Jonny McWilliams, for setting the whole thing up and being my mate....

And last but certainly not least, Judith Hannam for overseeing so many of my books now; you're a real pro and a pleasure to work with. However, Judith, there is only one slight problem... the football team you support.